IN LIKE FLYNN

BY

ART SCHAEFER

Art Schaefer

FOREWORD BY JOHN DAVIS

EDITOR: LAURA O'BAGY
GRAPHIC DESIGN: HANNAH HALEY MORRIS
PUBLISHER: MARY SCHAEFER
COVER: B-17 PAINTING BY MARY SCHAEFER
PRINTED IN U.S.A. BY ARIZONA LITHOGRAPHERS

FIRST EDITION
ISBN 0-9763182-1-0
MARYLSCHAEFER@COX.NET

Art in front of airplane "In Like Flynn".

IN LOVING MEMORY OF

JAMES D. LESTER
FRANK VAN VEENENDAAL
CLARENCE FAUBER
TIM BALLANTYNE

TABLE OF CONTENTS

FOREWORD
BY JOHN DAVIS

I came into this world during the darkest moments of WWII at about the same time the "Mighty Eighth", The United States Army's Eighth Air Force, came to being. It was the force that turned the tide of the European theater, shortened the war, and saved hundreds of thousands of lives. The Eighth Air Force has been referred to as "the greatest air armada of all time." I had the fortune of being placed in history at a time when all the men of my youth were heroes. These were the boys born of the 20's, Tom Brokaw's "Greatest Generation" who suffered from and learned to survive the greatest depression the world had ever experienced. When called, these young men left their jobs, studies, and families to make the world safe from oppression; they did this unquestionably for their love of country and their duty to fellow men and at great sacrifice to their loved ones who required their assistance to survive those toughest of times. I never knew these men's stories growing up, they didn't speak about the war or its horrors, I simply knew them as a breed of decisive, compassionate, and unselfish men who were wise beyond their years. As a youngster, in the presence of these men who were my teachers, scout masters and neighbors, I felt secure and assured that the future was mine.

When our servicemen returned home, they had aged an entire generation in just a few years. They experienced unspeakable horrors, many had been injured and maimed, and all had been subjected to work beyond exhaustion, and had carried out their responsibilities unfailingly, while in harm's way. These men attacked peace with the same passion in which they threw themselves into the war. They returned to school on the GI bill, married their sweethearts, raised families and applied their

experiences and learned discipline with the enthusiasm and ambition to create the greatest period of prosperity that the world had ever known.

As I grew older I learned that there were no greater heroes than the men of the Army Air Corps serving the European Operations. These were the young men who remained in school to earn the two years of college credit necessary to qualify and volunteer to fly over occupied territories, bringing the war to the enemy's home. They signed on knowing full well that it was statistically improbable that they would return home unscathed, with death or imprisonment much more of a certainty. How these young men barely out of their teens could climb into a B17 day after day meeting enemy fighters with their deadly track of tracers directed at them, passing through clouds of shrapnel explosions in the form of deadly grey and black puffs of smoke, and witnessing their comrades fall out of the sky is unfathomable, but they did it and without distraction to their mission. These were the heroes of my youth and even more today as I continue to learn about the men who stared into the face of fear and overcame their own while focused on their mission high over hostile territory.

Art Schaefer is that very special brand of hero, he's one of the young men who flew deliberately into the eye of the enemy and lived to tell, and he now shares with us the diary entries and reflections about his wartime experiences as a member of the 385th Bomb Group (heavy) Eighth Air Force, based at Great Ashfield, Suffolk, England. Coincidentally, this same group was activated in Art's home town of Tucson while he was pursuing his studies at the University of Arizona. We

are fortunate that Art's recollections are now preserved for us to understand and appreciate what our fathers and grandfathers had endured for the benefit of future generations. When I first asked Art about his experiences in the war he just said, "I was scared all of the time!"and not much more was forthcoming. I subsequently encouraged Art to write down his memories as a legacy for his children and grandchildren. But Art went well beyond that, and with the usual focus and precision of an engineer, he gathered photos, mementos, contacted former crew members or their surviving spouses and then put his findings and stories together for publication. Reading Art's recollections puts a humane and personal touch to the life and trials our servicemen experienced flying daily from the relative Safety of Britain, over the English Channel into occupied territories, and finally to the heartland of the enemy. As the navigator of the Flying Fortress "In Like Flynn," Art was that one person whom the B17 crew relied on to get them home safely when the plane made the turn after delivering its ordnance and completing its mission. Their plane was aptly named for Art's usual expression to let the crew know there was no doubt that he had found the safest course for home. Thanks to Art Schaefer, those wartime survivors, their families, and history enthusiasts everywhere now have an accurate and moving account of the daily life of men who flew from the fields of Britain.

Art Schaefer returned home to Tucson, Arizona, and completed his studies to become a mining engineer. Marriage to his sweetheart, Mary Esther, and a family came shortly thereafter, an accomplishment in itself since Art had advanced

to become a mining inspector overseeing more than 100 locations throughout North and South America. After fifteen years of constant moving, the Schaefer's permanently resettled in their beloved hometown of Tucson, Arizona. Mary, the love of Art's life later went on to become an internationally known floral and architectural artist. Her book,"The Life That Gave Me Art" (the double meaning is intended) chronicles her life and the travels of the wife of a mining engineer living in some of the most remote, primitive and sometimes most dangerous parts of North and South America.

Art and Mary are still as much in love as when they first met. They reside in a modest home that is renowned locally for its breathtaking and intricate floralscapes. Their life is filled with the joy of being close to their three children, grandchildren, and an untold number of friends and admirers.

If the reader has the opportunity to ask Art what kind of life he had, I'm sure that he'd smile and with that captivating twinkle in his eye, he'd just say "I was in like Flynn all the way."

PROLOGUE

My book *In Like Flynn* is from My Mission Diary of World War II that is an accurate documentation of every bombing or mercy mission I flew. The events you are about to read are made up of my memories I recorded immediately following each mission. They were on-the-spot documentations of each of my 33 combat or mercy missions. There were 27 combat missions and 6 Mercy missions. Each evening, after returning to my barracks, fit and thankful to be alive, and happy that the fear of having to "ditch" our plane in the North Sea was only temporary, I recorded the harrowing facts of the events of the day, to the best of my knowledge at the time. I did this so I would never, for the rest of my life, forget those events and the reasons why each was so important.

I have inserted actual pages of My Mission Diary that are in chronological order and followed by my more currently expanded memories of the war. I have also included additional stories, after the war years, to continue following the future lives of my crew, friends and family.

I was a young, totally indestructible, cocky twenty year old and filled with the feeling of wanting to serve my country. These were the feelings of patriotism and love of country that existed at the time and they belonged to our generation.

The movie about the "Memphis Belle", the first crew in the 8th Air Force to finish a tour, inspired me. It filled me with many emotions: love of country, comradeship, excitement and most of all, fear.

My book has given me an abundance of joy that I can share with my family and friends, and has brought new faces into my life that are eager to share their WW11 experiences with me. It has rewarded me with new friendships, all with a deep understanding of the times and a wish in their hearts to relive some of their own times and pals they once knew. It is my pleasure and wish to share with all, young and old, my memories, and feelings I have for the roles played by many others and myself in the Great War, and the pride we felt in being a part of the Greatest Generation.

PLEASE ENJOY!!!!

MY MISSION DIARY

By 1st Lt. Art Schaefer

THE CAVALRY

I began my military career in the horse cavalry ROTC at the University of Arizona. Our class of advanced ROTC training was the last class to have horses. When we left school they sold off the horses and dissolved the horse cavalry entirely.

As army reservists, we were sent to active duty at Fort Riley, Kansas for horse cavalry basic training while waiting for a cavalry officer's candidate school (OCS) to open up. When the cavalry school was closed, I transferred to the Army Air Corps and was sent to cadet training at Santa Ana, California. Following this I went to advanced navigator's school at Hondo just outside of San Antonio, Texas and after graduation, on to B-17 Staging in Tampa, Florida.

Our group always sang a lot so I will share this song with you.

Art in his Class A winter uniform in 1942–43.

The Cavalry Song

The cavalry's on the march

We're going to knock the starch

Right out of the enemy

And bring you to victory,

Each mom and dad will soon be glad

To welcome home the best son

Anybody ever had.

We're ready and set to go

And at the "Forward-Ho"

We're going to hit the road

And live up to our code.

Half as big, twice as tough

We're out to show the axis

That we really know our stuff!

As we go riding over every

Mountain trail

You'll hear us sounding off.

By the left flank-ho, by the right flank-ho!

In a million voices wherever we go,

We're going to get on the bit

And make the best of it!

Until the job is done and every-son-of a-gun

In the tanks or on the horses will agree

That we clear the highways for the infantry

And we're proud to be "The Cavalry".

BEFORE THE AIR CORPS
UNIVERSITY OF ARIZONA ROTC

*University of Arizona ROTC Class of 1944
singing at a dance in the Women's Gym in 1943.*

HIGH FLIGHT

Oh, I have slipped the surly bonds of earth

And danced the skies on laughter-silvered wings;

Sunward I've climbed and joined the tumbling mirth

   Of sun-split clouds—and done a hundred things

You have not dreamed of—wheeled and soared and swung

High in the sunlit silence. Hov'ring there

I've chased the shouting wind along and flung

My eager craft through footless halls of air.

Up, up the long delirious burning blue

I've topped the wind-swept heights with easy grace,

Where never lark, or even eagle, flew;

And, while with silent, lifting mind I've trod

The high untrespassed sanctity of space,

Put out my hand and touched the face of God.

John Gillespie Magee, Jr.

(Written by a 19-year-old American volunteer with the Royal
Canadian Air Force, killed in action December 11, 1941)

DEDICATION

I dedicate my book and my memories to my dearly beloved wife, Mary Esther and to my wonderful and loving children: Nancy, Cheri, Richard and their spouses, my grandchildren and great grandchildren. Mary's brothers, Ralph and Dick, share in our love and dedication; they also served their country with honor and bravery and always deserve to be remembered. I dedicate my stories to those who have enriched my life and will never be forgotten: to my parents, who instilled in me my strength in morals, respect and ambition to succeed, to my many loving friends who have traveled this life with me giving me much joy and support, and to my crew who will never be forgotten for I owe my life to them and many memories of life-long friendships. These are my beloved crew, brave and unforgettable. Many are gone but a few still live:

Clarence Fauber, Pilot

Dale Smeltzer, Co-pilot

Bill Schloss, Bombardier

Gerald Donnelly, Engineer

Jim Elder, Radio

John Demucci, Ball Turret Gunner

Walter Hatch, Waist Gunner

Bob Hake, Tail Gunner

Art Driscoll, Pilot I flew home with

To my buddy, Tim Ballantyne

Last but not least, thank you, John Davis, for having been my good and loyal friend who had offered endless encouragement and who gave me the "PUSH" and support I needed to write this book that's long overdue. To my dear friend, Laura O'Bagy, who has lovingly given her time and efforts toward my attempts to write this book and to edit and help it become a realization. Thank you, both of you, for seeing the importance of it for my family, my crew and for me!

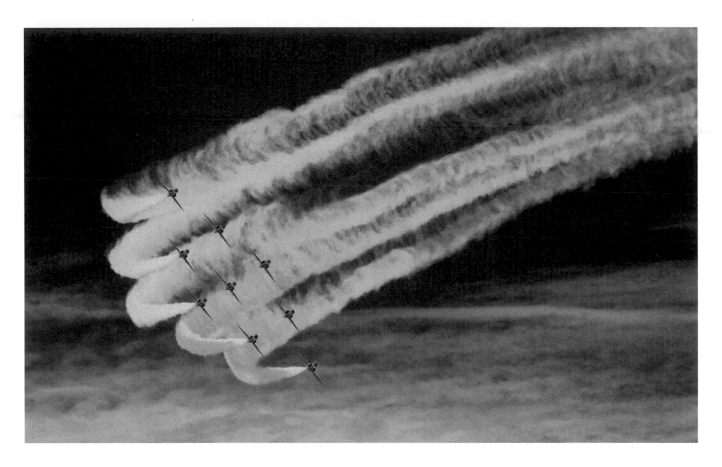

INTRODUCTION

In the month after the attack on Pearl Harbor, the United States Army's Eighth Air Force was established in Savannah. Less than a year later it was tasked with defeating the most powerful air force in the world, the German Luftwaffe. The Mighty Eighth took to the skies with the largest air armada ever assembled, flying daring daylight raids that eventually enabled the Allies to gain victory. Of the 350,000 Eighth Air Force airmen and ground personnel deployed to British airbases, 26,000 Eighth Air Force men would be killed in action, more than the entire U.S. Marine Corps lost in all of World War II. Another 28,000 would spend years in Nazi POW camps while 2,000 escaped.

HISTORY OF THE 385th BOMB GROUP

The 385th Bomb Group was founded in Tucson, Arizona in January of 1943. After training in Washington State, the Group joined the mighty Eighth Air Force in England in June and was based at Great Ashfield in Suffolk. From July 1943 to May 1945 (V-E Day), the group flew some 296 missions dropping over 18,000 tons of bombs on the continent of Europe. Many tons of food were also dropped into Holland in the "Operation Chowhound". Over 1,950 men completed tours and more than 1,400 were lost, either killed or missing in combat and crashes.

THE BOMBERS

Whenever I see them ride on high

Gleaming and proud in the morning sky

Or lying awake in bed at night

I hear them pass on their outward flight

I feel the mass of metal and guns

Delicate instruments, dead weight tons

Awkward, slow, bomb racks full

Straining away from downward pull

Straining away from home and base

And try to see the pilot's face

I imagine a boy who's just left school

On whose quick-learned skill and courage cool

Depend the lives of the men in his crew

And success of the job they have to do

And something happens to me inside

That is deeper than grief, greater than pride

And though there is nothing I can say

I always look up as they go their way

And care and pray for every one,

And steel my heart to say,

"Thy will be done."

By Sarah Churchill

MISSION DIARY

OF

LT. ARTHUR L. SCHAEFER

February to May, 1945

The cover to original mission diary.

549 SQUADRON, 385 BOMBARDMENT GROUP

THIRD WING, EIGHTH AIR FORCE

GREAT ASHFIELD, SUFFOLK, ENGLAND

385th Group Insignia

1ˢᵗ Lt. Art Schaefer Navigator

1ˢᵗ Lt. Clarence Fauber Pilot

PRAYER FOR A PILOT

Lord of Sea and Earth and Air,

Listen to the Pilot's prayer—

Send him wind that's steady and strong,

Grant that his engine sings the song

Of flawless tone, by which he knows

It shall not fail him where he goes.

By Cecil Roberts

LT. GEN. JAMES DOOLITTLE

Lt. General James Harold "Jimmy" Doolittle was the commander in Chief of the 8th Air Force in England the entire time that I was there.

He was a three-star general that had a great reputation in the Army Air Corps. He had led the raiders that bombed Tokyo early in the war and had a number of commands before taking over the 8th Air Force. He was awarded the Congressional Medal of Honor by Roosevelt for the Tokyo mission.

We were always very proud to have served under him as our commander.

But You Shoulda Seen the One That Tried to Get Away

U.S. Army Signal Corps Photos

It's no tall one, if Lt. Gen. Patton is describing to the boss the catch he expected to make beyond the Rhine. This bull session got in swing when Gen. Eisenhower visited the bridgehead at Remagen. Next to Patton in the 14-star photo is Lt. Gen. Bradley, 12th Army Group commander, with Lt. Gen. Courtney H. Hodges, 1st Army CG, at far right.

Allied Leaders from the Stars and Stripes Armed Forces newspaper, March 29, 1945.

IN LIKE FLYNN

Being the one crew member who always knew where we were, I pointed out places of interest as we traveled from Tampa, Florida, to England and then all over France, Germany, and Western Europe. When asked, I almost always told the crew where we were and what they were looking at.

However, many times I would be very busy and when they asked,"Where are we?" I would just say, "Don't worry, we're in like Flynn and everything is going to be OK." This got to be a joke with the crew. Anytime anyone asked, "Where are we?" one of the crew would come back with "Don't worry, we're in like Flynn."

Our crew had been assigned an old war weary B-17 named "Is This S-Trip Really Necessary?" It had been flown for a tour by the Pitts crew. We were finally given our own "Flying Fortress" a B-17 number 549, the same as our squadron. We called it "In Like Flynn."

Many years later my wife, Mary Esther, found some old World War II black- and-white photos that had yellowed over the years which were of our B-17. She painted an oil original of "In Like Flynn" for our 40th wedding anniversary as a present to me. I gave each of our crew members a large print of the painting. We, of course, have the original which I will always cherish and never part with. It has created much interest to the many who want to remember the "Big War" from a historical stand point or from their own past experiences. I hope Mary's painting and my book will help to retain the memories that stay near and dear to us as Americans.

ONE OF OUR LUMBERING BEAUTIES

"In Like Flynn", B-17 oil painting by Mary Schaefer.

Crew Chiefs for "In Like Flynn" airplane
Nemo Williams, Homer Krouse, Dodson.

Our Crew of In Like Flynn.

I WAS SCARED ALL THE TIME

Not long ago, I was talking to some friends about my experiences of flying over Germany in World War II. When I was asked, "Were you ever scared?" I answered truthfully, "Hell man, I was scared all the time!"

Over the years, I have learned that courage is not the absence of fear, but the overcoming of it. When we were flying, we all felt fear more times than I can remember, but bravado helped to hide it behind a mask of boldness. All of us showed fear in various ways at the same or different times. We were all "Flak Happy" from time to time, fortunately not all at the same time. Flak was the anti-aircraft fire from the enemy guns. The gunners in the waist, ball and tail of the aircraft were most susceptible to fear as was the bombardier because they were not as busy and had more time to ponder their vulnerability. They spent the entire time we were over enemy territory scanning the skies for bandits (enemy fighters) Messerschmidts, or Focke-Wulf 190s. The pilots, engineer, navigator and radio operator were always busy with their assigned tasks which kept them from worrying as much as those that had little to do to keep their minds occupied.

I recall being "Flak Happy" after the Dresden Mission, where we were attacked viciously by bandits, lost 25% of our squadron, and came close to having the entire squadron annihilated. After each briefing, I would pray that our mission would be scrubbed and we wouldn't have to fly. I gradually got over this feeling to some extent after flying well into my 27th combat mission. Most were less traumatic and eased any anxiety. We had a greater appreciation and awareness for life.

THE TWO-PERCENT THEORY

Once, while talking with Captain Marano, our Squadron Air Executive, I told him that when we first came to England as a replacement crew, we were told that we could expect 2% average losses on each mission flown. We did the math, figured that if we flew a tour of 35 missions, we had a 70% chance of not completing that number.

Captain Marano said something that I have remembered all my life. He said that the 2% figure is OK when things happen to other flyers, but if it happens to you, it is 100%!

From the Stars and Stripes Armed Forces newspaper April 12, 1945.

AN AIRMAN'S GRACE

Lord of thunderhead and sky

Who place in man the will to fly

Who taught his hand speed, skill and grace

To soar beyond man's dwelling place

You shared with him the eagle's view

The right to soar as eagles do

The right to call the clouds his home

And grateful through your heavens roam

May all assembled here tonight

And all who love the thrill of flight

Recall with twofold gratitude

Your gift of wings, your gift of food.

Father John MacGillivray, Royal Canadian Air Force

Art and Tim Ballantyne as new navigators in Tampa.

B-17 STAGING

After graduating from navigator school at Hondo, Texas, and receiving our wings and gold bars, Tim Ballantyne and I were assigned to B-17 bombers. We were sent to Tampa, Florida, for staging.

"Staging" consists of assembling various crew members from different training areas and melding them into a cohesive, workable crew. Our new crew met each other at Plant Park in downtown Tampa and was assigned to Drew Field, which was just west of town toward St. Petersburg. Tim met his crew and they ended up in the same barracks at Drew.

Our new crew was from all over the U.S. Our pilot and aircraft commander was 2nd Lt. Clarence E. Fauber, Jr. from East Chicago, Indiana. He was the only married member of the crew. His wife Maxine (Maggie) lived in a small apartment off the base. He was a third-year mechanical engineering student at Purdue University, and played in the school band. Later, he became a professor of engineering at Indiana State University at Terre Haute.

Our 1st co-pilot was 2nd Lt. Phillip Einsmann from New York City. Phil broke his wrist playing basketball, and was taken off our crew, put back for a few weeks and then assigned to a new crew. Our 2nd co-pilot was 2nd Lt. Dale G. Smeltzer from Boseman, Montana. He was a second-year Aggie student at Montana State University. Later he became a professor of agriculture at the University of California at Davis.

I was the navigator: 2nd Lt. Arthur L. Schaefer from Tucson, Arizona. I was a third-year mining engineering student at the University of Arizona and transferred to the Air Corps from the Horse Cavalry. I had played baseball and freshman football.

Our bombardier was 2nd Lt. William Schloss, from Cleveland, Ohio. He was second year student at Ohio State University. He had played freshman football for the Buckeyes.

Our engineer and top turret gunner was Sgt. Gerald Donnelly from St. Louis, Missouri. Later he became the 385th bomb group historian. He lived in Miami, Florida.

Our radio operator was Sgt. James Elder from Haverhill, Massachusetts. He was the oldest member of the crew at the age of 25. He now lives in Florida. Our waist gunner was Sgt. Walter Hatch from Duluth, Minnesota.

Our ball turret gunner was Sgt. John J. Demucci from Philadelphia, Pennsylvania. He was the smallest man on the crew and the only one that could fit into the ball turret. He had a girl friend named Marty that he later married. Our tail turret gunner was Sgt. Robert Hake, from Eaton, Ohio. He was the youngest member of the crew at age 19.

For three months we trained as a crew. We flew practice missions by ourselves and with small formations getting the feel of what to expect once we went overseas. We flew all over Florida and even pulled a land-fall on Havana, Cuba. Jim Elder suggested that we should have gotten overseas pay for this mission, especially since we were flying over shark-infested waters!

The Arizona Group at Hondo, Texas on Graduation Day at Navigator's School.

Art and Bill Schloss on leave in Tampa in class A uniforms.

Our new crew at Tampa.

OUR FIRST ESCAPE!

Shortly after getting our new co-pilot, we flew a night training mission. After navigating around south Florida in a planned route, we made a "bomb run" on Ocala.

With our required assignments completed, we returned to Tampa. Clarence Fauber, our pilot, told Bill Schloss and me that he would fly around Tampa for the remainder of our six-hour mission, and that we might as well go to sleep, which we did. Later, the pilot turned the controls over to our co-pilot and the pilot also went to sleep. He did not tell the co-pilot what the plans were.

The co-pilot, thinking that since we had a navigator to keep track of where we were all the time, he could just fly the airplane with no thought of staying around Tampa or keeping track of where we were. About an hour and a half later, the pilot woke up and asked, "Art, where the hell are we?" I had no clue!

Suddenly, wide awake, I took stock of our situation. Fortunately, it was a clear night and we could see the stars. I took a Polaris pole star, shot with my octant which I knew would give us our latitude. It showed us to be about 37 degrees North Latitude. We were in Georgia! I immediately gave the pilot a heading of due south and then computed a three star triangle fix with my octant. As I recall, I used Polaris again with Arcturus and Betelgeuse. It showed we were just north of Valdosta, Georgia, some 240 miles from our field in Tampa!

Fauber throttled back the engines to save gas and we headed home. We arrived an hour and a half late, just before they were sending out search planes for us. We landed safely, checked our gas gauges, and found we were flying on fumes. This was the first (and last time) I went to sleep while we were in the air!

Our crew in flying gear at Great Ashfield.

The crew clowning around in front of a red checkered board tail on our B-17.

WE GO OVERSEAS!

When we finished our staging training in B-17s at Drew Field, Tampa, Florida in mid-December, we were scheduled to go overseas to England and join the mighty 8th Air Force!

Tim Ballantyne's crew left for England immediately, but because two members of our crew had not had a leave for a year, we were all given two weeks leave over Christmas. I went home to Arizona, but my parents were living in California at the time because Dad handled the explosives, TNT, and dynamite, etc., for a big construction company. I spent Christmas with them and then returned to Florida about two days after Christmas.

Our first stop after leaving Tampa was Hunter Field at Savannah, Georgia. We were issued fur-lined jackets and other overseas clothing and were given a brand new Lockheed B-17 to deliver to England. We had to perform a number of test flights for the following reasons: the pilots had to check and calibrate their instruments; the bombardier had to check his Nordin bombsight; I had to calibrate all the navigation instruments; the engineer had to make sure the engines, gas tanks and other equipment were in good working order and the rest of the crew had to check their equipment. I recall calibrating the flux-gate compasses by flying along a railroad which we were told ran exactly due north and south for several miles.

We all went into Savannah a couple of times, but for some reason that weekend they closed the post so that only the field grade Major and above officers were allowed to leave the base. We made a quick trip to the PX and four very young looking "Majors" left the base on the bus that evening!

A few days later, we flew to Fort Dix, New Jersey, where we were weathered in for four days. Since our ball turret gunner, Johnny Demucci, lived in nearby Philadelphia, several of us accompanied him to his home to meet his family and girlfriend, Marty. I recall the great red wine that they served! We had a good evening and then went to midnight mass with the family. After the war, John married Marty and they have lived in Philadelphia and New Jersey ever since.

I don't recall where the rest of the crew went, but three of us, Clarence Fauber, Bill Schloss and I, took the train to New York City. We were in Times Square on New Year's Eve and participated in the festivities along with the hordes of people. We spent the night, what was left of it, in a hotel and went back to Fort Dix the next day by train.

The crew reassembled and flew from Fort Dix to Manchester, New Hampshire. Our radio operator, Jim Elder, lived in Haverhill, Mass., which was almost right on our way to Manchester, so we buzzed his house for some time, waving to his family and friends. Jim usually rode in the radio room amid ships where he had his office and desk, but for this trip he came up in the nose with Bill Schloss and me. From this vantage point he could see his house, family and friends on the ground.

Again, we were weathered in for several days in Manchester. We tried ice skating (for me it was the first and only time) and went sledding on the snow.

The next leg of our trip was to Goose Bay, Labrador, Canada. Once more, we were weathered in for four or five days. The base athletic officer was Captain Joe Sachen, whom I had known at the U. of A. He was a football guard and was the light heavyweight boxing champion of the U. of A. and the Border Conference. We became fast friends. He told me his brother was a POW of the Germans somewhere in Germany.

The snow was about 12 feet deep, so the two-story buildings only had one story visible. We played basketball, cards, and in the evenings, we sang all kinds of songs in the officer's club.

Clarence Fauber and another pilot were bragging about whose crew was the best. One thing led to another and before we knew it, we were challenged to a dogsled race. There were sleds but no dogs available so four of our crew members became "sled dogs" for the race. I was designated the "lead dog" for our team. Joe Sachen was the starter and judge. The pilots had names for all of their "dogs." I don't remember the names but I know that they were not too complimentary!

With the pilots as sled drivers, we mushed about 100 yards on the snow, turned around and mushed back to the starting line. There was a lot of cheering, jeering and harassing as we struggled from one end of the field to the other. We only fell down once while making the turn, but their team did too, so it was even. We won the race by half a length and proved, beyond a doubt, that we were the best crew!

The next morning, at 6:00 a.m. in the dark, they warmed our engines with big heaters, and we left Goose Bay, bound for Iceland by way of flying over Greenland. When flying over Greenland, everything looked the same, all white! As I recall, the highest mountain in Greenland is some 10,000 feet elevation, so we flew at 12,000 feet to be sure we didn't run into it. It was a boring trip, and at one time the whole crew was asleep except for Fauber and me.

After we crossed Greenland, we came down to about 6,000 feet. We could see the ice floes in the ocean and I got some good drift readings on them. We hit Reykjavik, the capital of Iceland, on the nose in the afternoon before it got dark which it did very early there in early January. There was very little snow. The wind blew the entire time while we were there. We waited for good weather so we could continue our trip. Iceland is a volcanic island and the airstrip was built on a big lava bed which was solid basalt!

Some of our crew members were billeted in the theater, which was a big multipurpose building with hardwood floors used for movies and basketball games. It had folding chairs for Sunday church services, dances, and meetings, etc. There were many cots arranged on the floor with a small table and folding chair for each man. The movie for that week was a western called, "Tall in the Saddle" with John Wayne and Jean Simmons. It was shown a half-dozen times each day. We all watched it several times until we knew all the words by heart! Some of the guys saw it 15-20 times.

We went into Reykjavik several times and everyone we saw was blonde. We didn't speak their language but were able to buy some tourist type things. Unfortunately the people were not too happy. Their homeland, Denmark, had been conquered and occupied by Germany. The Americans were using Iceland for an airbase to fly planes, equipment and troops to and from Europe and the U.S.A. One thing that impressed me was the short, stocky, shaggy Icelandic horses. We were told that in the winter these horses ate fish heads since there was no browse for them. In the summer they ate moss and grasses.

Finally, the weather cleared and we were able to take-off for the last leg of our trip. We left Iceland, flew to the northwest tip of Scotland and followed the western coast down to Wales. As we flew over Scotland, I identified Loch Lomond, and when I pointed it out to the crew, we burst into "You take the highroad, and I'll take the low road." Our crew sang a lot, both in the barracks and in the air! We sang songs for everything and everybody. Clarence taught us "Hail, All Hail to old Purdue," and "Indiana, My Indiana, Cream and Crimson," etc. For Bill and Bob we sang, "Fight the Team across the Field" which was for Ohio State. Dale came up with "It's Up with Montana, and down with the Foe." I had every one singing, "All Hail Arizona." Each of the crew had other favorite songs and we sang them all.

In one of the Scottish bays we spotted a warship! From our training course in "Aircraft and Naval Vessel Recognition," I identified it as the USS Texas battleship. Later, we learned that indeed it was the Texas, which had been damaged during D-Day landings and was in port for repairs.

We landed at Valley, Wales, on the Irish seacoast and were immediately relieved of our brand-new B-17, and put on a train and shipped to the replacement depot at Stone, Strafford, England, which was halfway between Liverpool and Leicester. We had completed our overseas journey and now were anxiously waiting to do our part for the war effort.

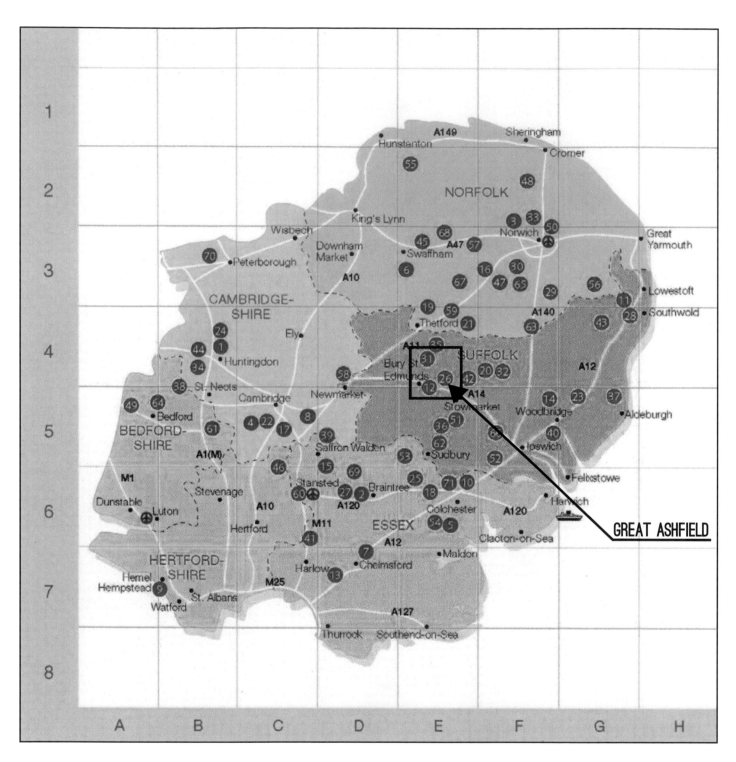

Airfields were located in East Anglia because this was close to the coast and had many farms and open country that could be used for air bases. The Eighth Air Force had some forty four B-17 and B-24 bases here.

COMBAT

We arrived at the 8ᵗʰ Air Force Replacement Depot (Repo. Depo) at Stone, England in mid-January. We were there, cooling our heels, waiting to be assigned to a combat group. Along with the B-17 crews there were B-24 and B-26 crews and fighter pilots here and we picked up a lot of new songs. We sang every evening around the piano, accompanied by crew members that played by ear.

I immediately contacted the Red Cross and asked if they could find where my hometown buddy, a fellow navigator, Tim Ballantyne was stationed. They checked and told me where he was based and that he had flown a mission over Germany the day before and was MIA (missing in action)! I thought, "Holy Cow, what have we gotten into?" Much later, I heard that Tim's plane was shot up, had lost an engine and landed in France at a fighter base. He didn't get back to his base until several days later. I found out which group he was with and was able to contact him after we were assigned to a combat group. His group was the 94ᵗʰ based at Bury St. Edmonds which was only 8 miles from our new group, the 385ᵗʰ, at Great Ashfield. We were able to see each other often, traveling by train, jeep, or bicycle. His pilot, Carl Dunn, was a good friend of Clarence Fauber, our pilot.

The 385ᵗʰ Bomb Group Heavy, was located at Great Ashfield, Suffolk in East Anglia. There were forty other American groups in the area, consisting of B-17s and B-24s. A train took us from Stone, with all our gear, through Cambridge, Bury St. Edmonds and letting us off at Elmswell, the little train station in the area. A truck met us and took us to our barracks which were Nisson huts, similar to our Quonsets, that were scattered around the base. We were "Eager Beavers," not too smart and maybe a little cocky, and wanted to fly missions right away.

The group had other ideas. We had more training to do such as practice missions over Scotland, gunnery practice, etc,. Our pilots were shown how to fly formation in combat over here, and the bombardier got all the new methods of bombing. We all shot skeet and generally kept busy getting ready. I learned how to use the British "Gee Box" navigation position finder as well as the local LORAN, which was the Long Range Aid to Navigation. We were told that these units worked great everywhere except over Germany where the Krauts jammed them, rendering them useless over enemy territory. We would have to rely on dead reckoning and pilotage for finding our where-abouts there.

One thing that our new group did that pleased our crew immensely was give all of our enlisted men promotions before flying missions. Their reason was that the Germans treated officers and sergeants much better than the corporals or privates if they were captured and made POWs.

When our crew was picked for lead crew training, we learned that as lead crew we would have the group commander, a squadron commander or other senior staff member flying as co-pilot. Our regular co-pilot would be in the tail gunner's position so he could keep all the airplanes in proper formation at all times. All the co-pilots took a dim view of these arrangements! Our crew was never called to be lead crew on a mission although we flew a number of times as deputy lead to take over in case something happened to the leader.

After a number of tests and supervised practice missions, our crew was selected for lead-crew training, which prolonged our entry into the war. Finally, however, we got to fly combat missions. Our pilot, Clarence Fauber flew first on February 16 as co-pilot with a seasoned crew. After that he was able to take our crew on regular missions. The Group bombed Wesel and the plane he was in was damaged by flak. They lost an engine and, not wanting to risk crossing the channel, landed in France.

The next day, I had my chance to fly. I flew with another seasoned crew. Our engineer, Gerry Donnelly, also flew his first mission with us. We were briefed to bomb a target almost to the Russian lines but were diverted to our secondary target just before crossing the battle lines in France. We bombed Frankfurt on Mainz. We saw our first flak, which was black smoke from the 88mm guns and white smoke from the 155 mms. Nobody suffered any serious damage and we returned home happy!

After a couple more missions with other crews, our crew flew our first mission together on February 23. It didn't go as planned. After take-off, we found that we could not get the wheels up, and by the time the engineer got them cranked up by hand, we missed our formation. We flew along the bomber stream looking for the big yellow tails with the square "G" but couldn't find them. The square "G" was our group's tail identification, a white square with a black G. This made it easier for the P-51 escort to identify us. We tied onto another group, which was the 547th and bombed with them. We hit a small town in the Nurmberg area and then stayed with that group until we reached France. We left them and came home alone to Great Ashfield.

385th Group airplanes on a mission over Germany. Photos by Bob Hake, our tail gunner.

SAV-385/34 4)(23-9-43)(3308-7-23600)(KERLIN-BASTARD)

Bomb strikes on German air base. From Squadron bulletin board.

The 385th on a mission to Berlin. Photo by Bob Hake, tail gunner.

(SAV-385°/1240-9)(11-APR-45)(46136-T-17500)(ENGOLSTADT)(TILT-6°-CONF)

Bomb strike photos showing results of bombs from each squadron (bulletin board).

On a mission over Germany. Photo by Bob Hake, our tail gunner.

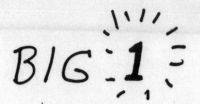

BIG 1

February 17, 1945

To: <u>FRANKFURT</u> "Little Magdeburg"

With Gerke's crew --- Lundstrom, co-pilot;
Wedmyer, bombardier and Gerald Donnelly,
engineer (our crew), etc.

Were briefed to go almost to the Russian
lines but were diverted just before crossing
the battle lines in France. No flak near
us within a quarter mile at least. Saw
some white flak from the 155mm guns.

20,000 feet over Hun land. Only two hours
in enemy territory, "Milk Run" the old boys
said.

Fauber flew his first mission yesterday
to Wesel and landed in France --- should be
home today.

I'M A COMBAT BOY NOW!!!!!!!!!!

(2)

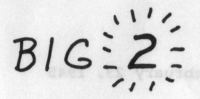

BIG 2

February 22, 1945

To: <u>ANSBACH</u> -- near Nurnberg

With Stenrose and crew --- Shank, co-pilot;
MacIntyre, togglier, etc. Supposed to hit
Zwickau, about 125 miles northeast.

    Went into dense clouds and lost our for-
mation over Germany. Came out of the clouds
at 17,000 feet, spotted some other group and
tied onto it.

    Bombed P.F.F. through the clouds,
could not see the ground. Never saw the
ground until we got back into France.
Followed the other group as "Tail End Charlie"
until we got well into France. Then left
them and came home alone. Skirted Dunkerque
where the Germans still hold a pocket of resistance.

NO FLAK --- Our Lucky Day!!!

Fauber flew as co-pilot with Pitts.

A helluva way to celebrate Wahington's
birthday!!

9 hours 20 minutes in air --- 4 hours over
Germany.

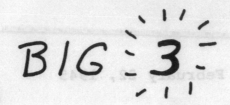

BIG 3

February 23, 1945

To: PFOFELD -- Small town in Nurnberg area

With own crew -- Crew's first mission together!!!

    After takeoff, we couldn't get the wheels up -- missed our formation. Flew along Bomber Stream for an hour looking for the big yellow tails with the square "G" but never found them.

    Tied onto the 547 Group and took a cook's tour of Germany for 4½ hours -- did not know what their target was, what the target ETA was, or anything.

    Saw flak at Merseburg and Chemnitz and almost hit while crossing the Rhine river on the way out. Bombed at 12,000 feet visually and blew hell out of the town. Saw 12 other towns hit in the same area.

Came back through France.

9 hours 35 minutes in the air --- 4½ hours over Germany.

 BIG-4

February 25, 1945

To: <u>MUNICH</u>

With Stenrose and crew again.

Visual target, did pilotage all over
Southern Germany and had a big time!!

Bombed marshalling yards, a bridge and
oil tanks. Other groups hit other parts of
Munich -- blew hell out of it!!!

Number 1 engine almost went out over the
target but we sweated it back into humming
again. Our luck holds out.

Saw Switzerland but couldn't persuade
the pilot to go there.

Saw some red flak (close) as well as a
lot of black.

One B-17 in the group behind us was hit
and blew up over target -- the biggest
pieces we could see falling were the engines.

Those Krauts aren't kidding!!!

9 hours and 30 minutes in the air.

(5)

BIG 5

February 26, 1945

To: <u>BERLIN</u> -- Big "B"

With own crew, except Mc Hugh flew in place
of Smeltzer as co-pilot.

Bill Schloss, our bombardier, got in his
first mission.

Bombed the target P.F.F. through the
clouds. Did dead reckoning navigation for
6 hours without seeing the ground once.
Wind up to 105 knots (about 120 mph) --
ground speeds coming home were 95 knots,
111 knots, etc.

Seven hours over Germany -- on oxygen!!

Over the target, Bob Hake, our tail
gunner comes up with: "Hold'er steady,
I'm taking pictures" -- with flak all over
the place -- these Krauts don't like us to
bomb Berlin, me thinks.

Saw Zuider Zee and flooded Holland
as well as the North Sea and a bit of Germany
on the way out.

Flew "Lenora Linda" airplane.

9 hours 20 minutes in the air.

(6)

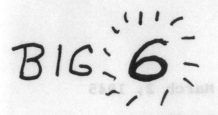

BIG 6 February 28, 1945

Air Medal Mission

To: <u>KASSEL</u> -- East of Cologne

With Wiess and crew -- Broughton flew as co-pilot.

Bombed P.F.F. through the clouds -- Flak heavy as hell, but low by the time we got there. Flew all over Frankfurt area and had a big time -- did dead reckoning, pilotage around the clouds along with Gee box -- Got a mustard cluster from the crew -- They were not used to having a navigator that knew where they were -- theirs kept getting lost!!!

McCarren (a navigator that went to school with me at Hondo) flew his first mission.

Saw some flying footlockers (B-24s) on the way home -- really sweat them out -- afraid they'd blow up!!

Only 7 hours 10 minutes in the air!

<u>I'm a hero now!!</u>

(7)

47

BIG 7

March 2, 1945

Bandits!!

To: <u>DRESDEN</u>

With Weiss and crew.

    Luffwaffe came up in force --
attacked from the rear in a company front --
out tail gunner counted 22 Focke-Wolfe 190s
in the first pass. They shot down 3 B-17s
from our squadron -- Tripp, Tipton and
Vaadi. Then they broke off and attacked in
pairs from 10:00 o'clock and 2:00 o'clock.
I thought sure as hell we'd had it.

    Our top turrent gunner shot down 3
FW 190s for sure, 2 maybe. I was shooting
my two flexible cheek guns and had a big
time. I got one probable and one damaged
FW 190. Saw pieces coming off wing roots
and fuselage as they went by. They were
close enough to shake hands with. Also shot
at 6 or 8 more. They were using 20mm cannon
that were only good inside of 400 yards --
we could shoot at them with our armor piercing incendiary 50 calibers while they were
way out -- and close up.

    Crew got 6 for sure, 5 probables.

    Came home above Frankfurt with a head
wind of 80 knots (about 91 mph) Chin turrent
gunner (togglier) shot the tail off of a 190
 at 1:00 o'clock -- confirmed!! Willie
Wilson -- bombardier in another plane got one
for sure, too. Chin Turrent gunner melted
his guns -- froze on the triggers, instead
of shooting short bursts. We were flying
number 2, so led the squadron home when we
lost our leader.   (8)

DRESDEN MISSION

On March 2, 1945, I flew a combat mission that we were not scheduled to fly to Dresden, Germany. Our crew was on stand down, but I was "asked" to fly with another crew whose navigator was in the hospital. Weiss was the pilot and we were flying in the low squadron.

Our primary target was a factory complex in Ruhland, Germany. I don't recall the secondary target, but the tertiary target and target of last resort was Dresden, in the event that we could not see the ground to find the first two targets. Dresden was a large city and we could pick it up with our radar, PFF (pathfinder force). The clouds were solid under us, and we never saw the ground after crossing the English Channel. It was impossible to see our first two targets so we headed for Dresden which was being bombed mercilessly by the British in retaliation for the Germans obliterating Coventry early in the war.

Dresden was full of civilians and soldiers who had fled Berlin fearing that they would be captured by the Russians. They preferred to fall into the hands of the Americans or even the British. They had gotten as far as Dresden when the British started their relentless bombing. The Germans even tried to move their capital from Berlin to Dresden but the British would have none of that and did everything they could to keep them from accomplishing this. An enormous number of Germans, mostly civilians, were killed in this operation. I have heard some 100,000 mentioned!

Somehow, our squadron became separated from the main group and we were out in the open by ourselves. We were sitting ducks! The Luftwaffe, quick to take advantage of our situation, came up in force. While one group of Bandits (German fighters) kept our escort P51s busy, another group made a pass at us. They formed what we called a "company front" formation. They were all in a line and came at us from the rear which made for a longer closure time. Our tail gunner counted 22 Focke-Wulf 190 and Messerschmitt fighters in line in the first pass.

They shot down three of our twelve planes in this pass. Our gunners in the back were all shooting as they approached. They went through our formation, broke off and attacked us in pairs from the front, at 10:00 o'clock and 2:00 o'clock. All of our gunners were shooting as each pair made their pass. I was shooting my two flexible 50 caliber cheek guns and had a big time. These were my first shots at an enemy in combat and I wanted them to count!

The Germans were shooting 20mm cannons that were only good inside of 400 yards or so, while we were shooting 50 caliber armor piercing incendiaries which we could use way out or close up. The Focke-Wulfs flew at us shooting and then, at about 50 yards or so, would flip over and go by us with their bellies facing us. This was where they had armor plates under the pilot's compartment. I put a short burst, as we were taught, right in the center of the belly of one fighter. He shuttered and seemed to go completely out of control. He went into a flat spin and disappeared into the clouds under us. If you don't see an enemy plane blow up or crash into the ground, you don't get credit for a "kill." I was credited with a "probable" with him.

I hit another Focke-Wulf with a short burst and saw big pieces coming off the wing roots where they were attached to the fuselage. The plane continued on with no obvious control problems. I was credited with a damaged FW190 for this one. Our crew claimed 6 kills and 5 probables. Our bombardier, shooting his chin turret guns, shot the tail off a FW190 at 1:00 o'clock and got a confirmed kill. I shot at some 10-12 bandits over a period of half an hour or so and had a big time!

One good thing about having the bandits after us was that there was no flak! Fighters were much more dangerous than flak, but at least we didn't have both to contend with. Our lead bombardier was on the ball and we salvoed our entire bomb loads right in the big middle of Dresden.

With all the distractions of the battle, all of our navigators lost track of where we were. Our Gee Box and other position locators were useless because they were jammed by the Germans. Fortunately for us, we passed a small hole in the clouds and we could see the ground for just a moment. It was the only time we saw the ground all day! I was able to identify a pilotage point, the town of Coburg, Germany, in that short time. Our pilots were on the radio talking with each other and they all asked: "Does anybody know where we are?" Since I did, we were immediately designated the squadron leader. We led the squadron back to France.

We were bucking a head wind of 80 knots (about 91 mph) most of the return trip. We hit the no-flak corridor above Frankfurt and encountered no more enemy action.

My own crew, back at Great Ashfield, heard about our battle and knew we had lost several planes, but did not know which ones. They were out at the control tower to welcome us home: Clarence Fauber, Bill Schloss, Gerry Donnelly, John DeMucci and Bob Hake were all anxiously waiting for our planes to land. They were as happy to see me as I was to see them! The group lost four planes, our three plus one from one of the other squadrons. This was my 7th combat mission. I never forgot Coburg.

B-17 going down in flames. No chutes visible.

Q. Why is practically nothing ever said in any history of World War II about the destruction of Dresden? Didn't Churchill goof on that one?—L. H., Denver, Colo.

A. In February 1945, British and American bombers flew over Dresden, 70 miles behind the Eastern front in Germany. The city was undefended. In addition to its own population of 630,000, Dresden then contained 500,000 refugees fleeing from the advancing Russian armies. The Allied bombing, largely British, burned out the city, killed 135,000 people. This is more than the number of Japanese destroyed by the first atomic bomb dropped on Hiroshima. Says Churchill: "The destruction of Dresden remains a serious query against the conduct of Allied bombing."

Winston Churchill's remarks about The Bombing of Dresden.

 **BIG 8**

March 10, 1945

To: <u>SOEST</u> -- "East of Happy Valley"

With Fauber and our own crew.

Flew to 7 degrees 30 minutes east past the Zwider Zee, lost an engine, salvoed our bombs in Germany and came home alone.

Two P-51s escorted us back to England -- even tapped our wings to reassure us and did acrobatics all the way home. I love those peashooter jockeys!

One rack of bombs hung up in the bomb bay so we brought them back with us. Bill Schloss and I sweat out the landing but it was damn good.

Added note: Mission did not count -- Group orders!!! So only have in seven.

Fauber forgot the colors of the day - for flares to identify us as Americans to the 51s - had a hard time convincing them we were friends. I tried blinker on one but I think he must have flunked that course.

(10)

THE SOEST MISSION

On March 10, 1945 our group flew a mission to Germany. We were briefed for a target in Soest, a town about seventy five miles northeast of Cologne on the eastern edge of Happy Valley (the Ruhr). We flew over Holland, saw the Zuider Zee (sea) and then into Germany. We were well into Germany when we started having troubles with two of our engines and were having a hard time keeping up with our group's formation.

We were some seven degrees, thirty minutes east longitude, approximately 450 miles from England, and about thirty minutes from the target when one of the engines went out. We quickly decided to abort the mission and return home alone. Rather than feathering the faulty engine, (stopping the propeller and turning the blades into the wind) Fauber elected to let it windmill (letting it to turn powerless in the wind). A feathered propeller was a sure signal to the bandits (enemy aircraft) that we were in trouble and would then make us a tempting target. From a distance, a windmilling propeller appeared to be functioning properly.

We contemplated our return home. We were several hundred miles inside Germany and still had Holland and the North Sea between us and safety. We knew that the Luftwaffe, the German Air Force, loved to hop onto lone bombers in distress.

A minute or so later, our top turret gunner, Jerry Donnelly announced, "We have company." We saw two P 51s, one on each side of us and we knew we had an escort home to safety. PRAISE THE LORD! One even tapped our wing with his to reassure us that they were truly excellent pilots and that we were in very good hands! They even did a few acrobatics for us, putting us in a more positive mood and in a lighter frame of mind. We applauded them with the deepest appreciation, and I'm sure they saw us.

We continued safely on our way, even though we were bucking a headwind of some eighty miles an hour. On our way we dropped our bombs on a target of opportunity in Germany, hitting a small industrial town. One rack of bombs hung up in the bomb bay. The bombardier and radio operator tried to dislodge them while we were still over Germany, but they were unsuccessful. We decided to bring them back with us.

We made the no-flak corridor over Holland and continued out into the North Sea. Since we were out of range of the Luftwaffe bandits, the pilots of our "Little Friends" (the P51s) waved goodbye, did a couple of barrel rolls in front of us and headed home to their base in France.

We got back to Great Ashfield with our three good engines and had no more troubles. We sweated out the landing because of the hung-up bombs but our pilot Clarence Fauber made a perfect landing.

We did not get credit for the mission because we did not hit the intended target (Squadron orders).

Our "Little Friend" P-51 that escorted us when we lost an engine and came home alone from Germany. Photo by Bob Hake.

THE MISSION

Edgar Allen Schmoe
(as told to Art Schaefer and Adapted from
Edgar Allen Poe's, "The Raven")

Once upon a mission dreary

While of combat I'd grown weary

I had flown a thousand hours

And was sure to fly some more,

When suddenly I heard a knocking

Sounded like some flak a popping

Popping like the very devil

Just beneath my bomb bay door,

Tis some Jerry quickly thought I

Wishing to improve his score,

I will use evasive tactics

Even if he does get sore.

Turning then, I saw before me

Blacker yet than ere before

Flak abursting close and heavy

Guess I'd better turn some more

Then I opened wide my bomb doors

And, to my surprise and horror

Flashing fast and bright beneath me

Were some ninety guns or more.

And above the shrapnel shrieking

I remembered that at briefing

They had told us with much speaking

There were only three or four.

Leveling then I made a bomb run

Which was not a very long one,

For the varsity was on duty

And I'd seen their work before.

When an engine coughed and clattered

And the glass around me splattered

And I knew they had my number

Just my number, nothing more.

I had lost my upper turret

And alone, defenseless, worried

I was then the saddest creature

Mortal woman ever bore.

While outside, like ducks migrating

Was a drove of M.E.s waiting

Waiting all with itching fingers

Just to even up the score

And each bright and streaming tracer

Coming nearer, ere nearer

Made my spirit sink within me

Just my spirit, nothing more.

But at last to my elation

I caught up with my formation

And the M.E.s turned and left me

By the tens and by the score

But my wings were torn and tattered

And as far as I'm concerned

My nerves were shattered

Just my nerves and nothing more.

Now, I've found the joy of living

And this secret I am giving

To all of you and those

Who would care to give some more

For my sinus starts to seeping

Every time they mention briefing

No more flying, no more combat

No more missions, nevermore.

BIG 9

March 12, 1945

To: SWINEMUNDE -- On the Baltic Sea.

With Shank and our crew except Fauber in
airplane number 549 (same squadron).

In Like Flynn

Very good mission.

Did pilotage over Denmark, saw Sweden
and the Baltic Islands.

Bombed invasion barges the Huns were
going to use to clear out of Stettin Bay.
Also bombed the Admiral Scheer pocket battleship that was in the harbor. Carried six
1000 pound bombs.

Light flak from big guns but bombed
P.F.F. through the clouds and they couldn't
see us. No Luffewaffe fighters -- praise
the Lord!!!

Saw lots of enemy ships above Kiel
including 2 submarines, several mine sweepers
and one big ship.

Bill and I had a big time on the way
back listening to the radio and playing
" Who Dat" with other planes in the group.

8 hours 20 minutes in the air.

(11)

BIG-9- again!

March 20, 1945

To: <u>HAMBURG</u> -- Visual!

With Shank and own crew.

Flew in 6 ship formation high over high
ahead of the group as chaff ships. Carried
forty 100 lb. practice bombs full of chaff
(strips of tin foil on paper) to foul up
the German radar on the flak guns.

Really buzzed over Hamburg at 170mph
indicated Air speed -- about 300 mph
ground speed -- about 31,000 feet altitude
which didn't make me feel bad!

Intense flak and very accurate --
did a lot of evasive action but group
caught hell -- those Kraut master sargents
were fairly zeroed in! Fighter scare on
way out. 3 jet fighters -- ME210s -- made
a pass at us but nobody was hit.

Flak on way out damn accurate --
Stenrose hit -- lost #3 engine and had the
top turret hit -- Fauber was flying as
co-pilot. They came home alone and made
it okay.

Almost everybody got hit a little
but we didn't lose anybody. We got a few
holes in our tail. Flew Pitt's ship,
<u>"Is This Strip Really Necessary ?"</u>

6 hours 30 minutes in the air.

<u>Tough Mission!!!</u>

We led the 8th (12) today

WE CROSS THE RHINE

After D-Day, the Allies liberated France and were slugging their way toward Germany. In March 1945, they ran into a natural barrier—the Rhine River. This barrier had to be overcome for the Allies to continue their attack on the German homeland. This was a joint American-British airborne operation that took place toward the end of World War II. Involving more than 16,000 paratroopers and several thousand aircraft, it was the largest single airborne operation in history to be conducted on a single day and in one location. The Germans had concentrated a large number of defenses on their side of the river. They were dug in and determined to keep the Allies from breaching this barrier.

All the bridges over the river were destroyed, bombed by our 8th and 9th Air Forces or blown up by the German army as they retreated.

March 24, 1945, was the date set for crossing the Rhine, called operation "Thunder." These preparations were made well in advance. Our army engineers had to plan their pontoon bridges and bring all the equipment near our side of the river. Gliders would be used to transport many troops over the river and behind the German defenses. The glider pilots would take a number of troops over with their weapons and other war equipment, and then join them in the battle. Many paratroopers would jump behind the German lines also. The main body of ground troops, tanks, etc., had to be made ready to cross. The 8th and 9th Air forces and the RAF were asked to help out all we could. This entailed softening up the German defenses on the east side of the river. We started well in advance because a large number of targets would be hit for several days up to the crossing time. On March 21, our group bombed a German fighter plane base at Zwischenahner near Oldenburg. We wanted to be sure the Germans couldn't use it to put up fighters to attack our troops. Base buildings were destroyed and the runways were left full of bomb craters. We thought this mission was great. There were no bandits, no flak, and we were only in the air a little over four hours, a big milk run!! The RAF was really doing their part. We saw a group of their Lancasters going in as we were on our way out of Germany. They flew formation like turkeys, but we were sure happy to see them joining us in this operation.

The next day, March 22, flying in the plane called "IS THIS S-TRIP REALLY NECESSARY", we bombed Ratingen, a small town in "Happy Valley" which was the Ruhr Valley about 30 miles north of Cologne. The weather was clear, we bombed visual, and for us at a low altitude of 24,000 feet, instead of our usual 28,000 to 30,000. This produced better bombing results but also greatly improved the flak accuracy. We were only over German lines about seven minutes, but what a rough seven minutes! Our group really caught HELL from the flak guns.

Sixty of them tracked us from the time we crossed the Rhine back to the Rhine and they were too damn accurate. One of our B-17s, "Closz Call", named for their pilot, Lt. Closz, had an 88 mm projectile go through the wing but it didn't explode or they would have had it! 88s explode by preset altitude, not impact. Another B-17, "Hot Chocolate" had a runaway engine over the target, but got the propeller feathered OK with the blades stopped and turned into the wind. Our number 3 engine was hit, disabled and set on fire. Our pilots and engineer were really on the ball and got it under control in one minute flat and extinguished the fire. We came home alone on the three engines. Everybody suffered some battle damage. Our luck continued to hold out! This was one of our toughest missions.

The next day, March 23, flying a different airplane, "Angels Sister", we went to Siegen, another town in "Happy Valley." It is about 40 miles from the Rhine, almost due east of Cologne. Again, it was a clear day and the flak was accurate but not as intense as the day before. Flak blew the tail off of a B-17 in the group ahead of us. It went down and took another plane with it. They both crashed about ten miles behind the lines. We saw a few parachutes but couldn't tell how many guys got out. We saw targets burning all over the place. We really leveled the vicinity for some time to come. The 8th and 9th air Air Forces and the RAF were really pounding this area.

On the big day, the crossing of the Rhine on March 24, our group was scheduled to fly two missions in support of our troops' crossing. Flying our own airplane, "In Like Flynn", our first target was the fighter base at Zwischenahner again. The Germans had rebuilt the runways. This mission was routine, without flak or attacks by bandits. It was another Milk Run, thank the Lord. We saw the big smoke screen blowing across the river and hundreds of Allied gliders on the enemy side of the river. They had ferried our troops over the river to landings in fields or any other open spaces. They were piled up in some of the fields like grasshoppers or cicadae under a street light. Our crew was scrubbed for the afternoon mission, I don't remember why. I don't recall if the rest of our group crews flew or not.

The crossing of the Rhine was the beginning of the big push into the German Homeland and was a turning point in the war. When it was over, we were all glad that we had participated in this momentous operation, but it sure didn't help our life expectancy much! We were all happy to be alive!!

While flying our tours, we were awarded three battle stars on our ETO medal ribbons. As I recall, these were the Battle for Rhine Land, Central Europe, and Aradennes. These battles helped bring the war to a successful end for the Allies.

The operation was the last large-scale Allied airborne operation of World War II. It was the largest airborne operation in history, and will never be repeated!!

BIG 10

March 21, 1945

To: <u>ZWISCHENAHNER</u> -- near Oldenburg

With Shank and own crew.

Were ground spare but took off late and caught formation in the middle of the North Sea -- Really sweat out joining the formation because we were flying an old dark painted ship. (The Germans were known to use captured B-17s painted black to track our formations). All the gunners in the group were tracking us until we joined the formation.

Flew visual over Germany, bombed a jet airfield near a lake -- blew hell out of it and came home over Holland. No flak, no fighters -- only 4 hours 3 minutes in the air!!! Big Milk Run!!!

Saw RAF going in as we were on our way out -- flew formation like turkeys! But I guess those flying bombbays are O.K.

Our ball turret didn't work but we didn't need it so......... DeMucci flew in the waist with Hatch.

(13)

63

BIG 11

March 22, 1945

To: <u>RATINGEN</u> -- in "Happy Valley"

With Fauber and our crew.

    Visual -- but only over German lines about seven minutes -- but what a rough seven minutes!!! 60 flak guns tracked us from the Rhine back to the Rhine and those master sargents were sure checked out. Had to feather one engine on fire over target -- got it under control in one minute flat!! Plane in front of us -- "Close Call" -- got an 88mm shell through his wing but it didn't explode or he would have had it!! (88s go off by altitude, not impact). "Hot Chocolate" had a runaway prop but got it feathered O.K.

    Came home alone over North Sea -- 6 hour mission. Flew Pitt's ship. "Is This Strip Really Necessary."

(14)

BIG 12 March 23, 1945

To: <u>SIEGEN</u> -- in "Happy Valley"

With Fauber and crew.

    We hit the blue, flew over Rhine River
and took a bomb run on the Rhur but lead
Bombardier messed up so we hit Siegen instead.
Visual all the way -- saw a big smoke screen
along Rhine.

    Saw flak blow the whole tail off a B-17
in front of us -- he went down in flames and
took another plane with him which crashed
about ten miles behind the lines -- <u>they had
it</u>!! Flak was light but accurate!!

    Saw targets burning all over the place --
we really about leveled that vicinity for
sometime to come!

    Flew "Angel's Sister"

    Bill's air medal mission -- my first
cluster to it.

    7 hour mission!!

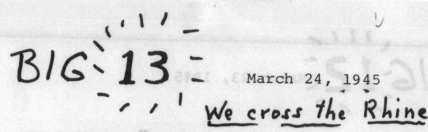

BIG 13 March 24, 1945

<u>We cross the Rhine</u>

To: <u>ZWISCHENAHNER</u> again!!

With Fauber and Crew --

We cross the Rhine. Bill was o.g. and didn't get to go, but I wore his "50 mission" hat for luck. Almost missed mission, took off late and met formation at Dutch coast.

Saw thousands of planes blowing hell out of everything in the area that was worth bombing -- hit our target right on the button!!

Visual -- could see 50 miles -- but no flak, no fighters and only 4 hours and 10 minutes in the air -- I'd like about 22 more just like it!!

Saw a helluva lot of gliders and a big smoke screen from Happy Valley.

Flew 549 again. I guess the big push is on!!

We named it "IN LIKE FLYNN!"

(16)

BIG 14

March 28, 1945

To: <u>HANOVER</u>

With crew in "Is This Strip Really Necessary?"
again.

    Assembled over France -- had to climb
thru 18,000 feet of clouds on instruments
before breaking out. Contrails so thick
we had to keep going higher to stay over
them. Flew over Germany going from one
formation to another -- finally bombed
with lead Sqdn. -- 17 other ships did, too!!
Heavy flak in front of us but was low when
we got there -- lucky us!!

    Came home by Dummer Lake and almost got
lost going thru clouds but came home with
formation O.K.

    Sweat out landing -- ¼ mile visibility!!!

    0720 hrs. in air.

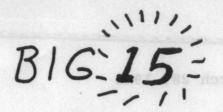

BIG 15 March 30, 1945

<u>Good Friday</u>!!

To: <u>HAMBURG</u> -- visual!!

In "Is This Strip Really Necessary?"

No air speed meter -- no flux-gate compass,
number 3 engine out -- but flew her to the
target -- saw more flak today than I've
seen for quite awhile -- really in there!!
But Fauber's evasive action was too much
for those master sergeants!!

Flak bounced off top turret but nobody
hurt. Came home alone by Kelly's constant
and gee fixes -- God, even Helgoland shot
at us on the way out!! Number 2 engine
almost out over target --2 B-17s blew up
ahead of us but four chutes got out of one.

Came thru snow storm on way home --
had lightening playing around wing tips
and nose -- had one inch snow on right
cheek gun when we broke out.
St. Elmo's Fire!

The boys who were sweating today were
us!!!

We led the 8th. A.F. today. Col. Jumper
led mission.

Famous saying: "Sir, can I come out and
get a smoke? I'm a <u>little</u> nervous! <u>Ball
Turret</u>!, John DeMucci.

08:00 hours in air.

(18)

BIG 16

March 31, 1945

Easter Eve!!

To: <u>BRANDENBURG</u> -- 30 miles from Berlin!!

In: "Queenie" -- Is This Strip Really Necessary?"
Our ship now!!!

   Flew over battle lines into target --
about nine tenths coverage all the way. Did Gee
box and D.R.

   Bombed thru clouds -- no flak -- but got a
good flak pilotage point going in -- shot up
a "Scarecrow" -- big black burst that looked
like a 16 in. gun at least!! Saw a Nazi jet
plane with about nine P-51s on his tāil --
hope they got the s.o.b.!

   Came home over Holland and had a big
time tearing home at 200 mph indicated air
speed.

   Turboes om the blink, but made it O.K.

   Should bomb a church tomorrow!!

   0800 hr. mission. We were tail-end
Charlie today.

BIG 17

April 4, 1945

To: <u>KIEL</u> -- Baltic Port

With: Kitsz and crew of 551 squadron.
Poorly disciplined crew!!

Had a hard time finding plane -- we had
3 different ones before we took off!
Took off late but got into formation over
Buncher 13 before we left England.

Saw a midair collision in our lead
squadron -- Crimmens and Richie both went
down -- 1 man got out but was dead when they
found him!!

Bombed thru clouds but saw target after
bombs away -- blew hell out of those sub-
pens! I think the whole Hun Navy was in the
bay -- hope we hit a few ships, tho.
Saw some red flak and lots of black but we
didn't get hit!

Group next to us got shot up by flak over
Denmark but we made the corridor good --
Hell, we even missed Helgoland, too!!

0700 hours in air.

Carried 6 - 1000# bombs.

Crimmens last words:
"Clambake Leader - we are
aborting"

(20)

BIG 18 April 7, 1945

To: <u>GUSTROW</u> -- Northern Germany

With Fauber and crew in "Queenie".

Luffwaffe came up in force -- we saw
2 Me 109s, about 4 jets close and about 8
more way out -- the Pee-shooter boys were
really in there pitching and we lost only
one plane -- midair with an Me 109!

At I.P. a B-17 went down but the crew
bailed out O.K.

Hit an Ordance plant and blew hell out
of it -- one late release hit an ammo dump
in woods.

One Me 109 came thru formation trying
to get away from a P-51 but I'm afraid it
didn't do much good. Also saw a fighter
shot down in front of us. Really had our
crew on that old ball today.

<u>Now the Huns can't tell their arsenals
from a hole in the ground!</u>

Bombed at 15,000' visual.

08:30 hrs. in air.

12 - 500# bombs.

(21)

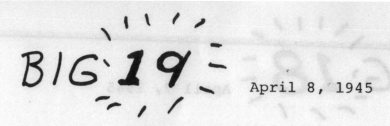

BIG 19

April 8, 1945

To: <u>HOF</u> -- Helping Patton!!

With: Fauber and crew in "Queenie".

Flew at 5,000 over France --
Bombed at 15,000' -- briefed for no flak --
but an 8 gun battery knocked hell out of a
few of the boys -- not from our group, tho.

Saw four B-17s go down,three at the
target - 1 later - but saw total of 22
chutes from four -- could've been more!!

Flew right by Nurnburg but couldn't stop.
Hit marshaling yard -- blew hell out of it!!
Visual - 6- 1000# bombs.

08:20 hours in air.

Saw Rhine River valley where Patton and
Patch crossed.

April 9, 1945

To: NEUBURG -- Near Munich

With Fauber and crew in "Queenie".

Flew over Munich but got cut out by another squadron just before bombs away and had to go to Neuburg. Almost had it! We were stalling out in prop wash above Closz at the target but Co-pilot saved the day.

Saw three B-17s go down -- one blew up at the target, one went out of control, did a loop, two split S-s and then crashed -- no chutes!!

Came back over Maunheim, Rhine river and Little Maginot Line in Belgium. Saw Brussels and a lot of beat up Germany. A B-17 crashed by Rhine and flares were flying all over the place like mad.

(23)

BIG 21   April 10, 1945

To: <u>NEURUPPIN</u> -- 30 miles from Berlin

With Fauber and crew in "Queenie"

    Bombed airfield and barracks, no flak
at target but had the hell shot out of our
low squadron --Holmes lost engine but led
home O.K. -- over Stendal by 6 gun railroad
battery at 15,000' Joy Dunlap had major
battle damage but made it O.K.-- Piechotties
34th. mission!!! Saw two B-17s go down behind
us but we didn't lose anybody -- saw Berlin
in distance -- crossed battle lines near
Hanover -- Monty and Simpson battling the
Krauts here. Saw about a thousand gliders on
East side of Rhine -- Osnabruck is really
beat to hell -- level it was!!!

(24)

BIG 22   April 11, 1945

To: <u>INGOLSTADT</u> -- on Danube

With Fauber and crew in "Queenie".

    Bombed marshalling yard with trains
in yards -- blew hell out of it!!

    Flew along Blue Danube -- but it was
<u>green</u>! But saw a lot of beautiful country --
just north of Munich.

    Bill flew as navigator -- talked to him
over command -- Peanuts to Hotnuts -- he
flew with Wiloughby.

    Carried 6 - 1000' bombs.

    No flak, no fighters -- big milk run --

    Helped Patton again.

Art in front of airplane "In Like Flynn".

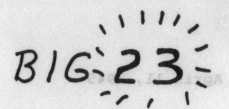

BIG 23   April 16, 1945

To: <u>BORDEAUX</u> -- French Port! *Royan*

With Fauber -- Anderson, Co-pilot and crew
in "Queenie"

    Bombed at 15,000', 6 - 1000# bombs on
German pocket of resistance holding the port
of Bordeaux -- the French are trying to take
it -- saw LeHarve, CherbourgPenn, Man-made
port, and a helluva lot of France. Over
enemy territory for 30 seconds! No flak,
no nothing!! Big Milk Run! I even flew
Co-pilot in formation for awhile on the way
home!

    I now have four combat minutes of stick
time!! Would like 12 more like it!

ROYAN MISSION

On April 16, 1945, our crew flew a mission to Royan in the Port of Bordeaux, France to bomb a German pocket of resistance holding the Port. It had been bypassed by the Allies when they liberated France after D-Day on June 6, 1944. The French army was trying to take it back from the Germans.

We carried six P-51 gasoline tanks full of Napalm (jellied gasoline) with igniters to start fires all over the area. Napalm had been used in bombing Japan and proved very effective. We worried about carrying these things on our plane. The whole plane reeked of gasoline and we had a no smoking rule which everybody complied with.

There was no flak or bandits to worry about. We bombed at 15,000 feet which made for increased accuracy and damage on the ground. We were over enemy territory only 30 seconds! This was a big milk run. I even flew co-pilot in formation for awhile on the way home. I now have four combat minutes of stick time.

We saw a lot of France. We saw Normandy, LeHarve, Cherbourg Peninsula and all the places where the Allies landed on D-Day, German fortifications, a man-made port used by the Allies and other French sites.

We were told not to mention that we had used Napalm on the Germans. I even wrote in my log and diary that we carried six 1000- lb. bombs that mission! Only after the war in Europe ended were we allowed to talk about this.

Artist Richard Schaefer, my grandson

MY "ALMOST" PURPLE HEART

On my 4th Mission, I flew with Arnold Stenrose's crew to Munich, Germany. It was clear and visual all the way so I could use pilotage (looking at the ground) all over Southern Germany and I was having a big time. Our group bombed marshalling yards, a bridge and oil tanks—we blew hell out of all the targets.

While the clear weather improved our bombing accuracy, it also improved the German flak gunners' accuracy and we caught some close ones. One B-17 in the group behind us blew up—the biggest pieces we could see falling were the engines. Everybody got hit a little. One close burst sent shrapnel through our nose, and a piece about the size of a nickel hit me in the chest. Fortunately, I always wore my big heavy flak suit when we were over our target and the flak didn't go all the way through. I was knocked head-over-heels into the catwalk between the nose and the pilot's compartment. I reattached my oxygen line and throat-mike and continued navigating. I had a big bruise on my chest and was sore for a week. Otherwise, I was none the worse for this experience.

This was as close to getting a purple heart that I came. If I had reported it, I probably could have been awarded one; instead, I flew with my own crew the next day to bomb Berlin.

SILVER SHIPS

There are trails that a lad may follow

When the years of his boyhood slip,

But I shall soar like a swallow

On the wings of a silver ship,

Snug in my coat of leather

Watching the skyline swing,

Shedding the world like a feather

From the tip of a tilted wing.

Mildred Plew Meigs

GERMAN MUNITIONS FACTORY

In early February 1945, our crew, Lt. Clarence Fauber's of the 549th Squadron, flew a mission to Munich, Germany. I was the navigator. The weather was beautiful, we could see our targets visually and we destroyed some marshalling yards, a bridge and oil storage tanks. Our escort, the P-51s, were on the ball, and we had no attacks by "bandits" (German fighter planes).

Heading back to France and home to England, I was noting the patterns of forests on the ground between Augsburg and Neu Ulm. Our navigation maps were very exact and showed the shapes and sizes of the forests. With the eyes of a hunter one group of trees caught my eye—things just didn't look right with it—some of the trees looked too patterned and of slightly different colors. The way the railroad tracks entered and exited the forest did not seem right either. A small road entered the forest, but none came out. I pinpointed the location on my map, entered the co-ordinates in my log and reported my observations to our de-briefing team at Great Ashfield when we landed.

On following up several days later, I was told that the British had sent two Mosquito fighter bombers over to check the place out. They saw what I had noticed and bombed the area. All hell broke out—the explosions were about 10 times what would be expected from the bombs dropped. It turned out that this was an underground munitions factory. They manufactured ammunitions: 88, 105 and 150mm flak shells, 20mm cannon shells, and 9mm rifle and machine gun cartridges for the German armies. The British later returned and completely destroyed the factory.

Our crew received a "Thank You" from the group and the 8th Air Force Headquarters and I was awarded an extra Air Medal for being so observant.

THE RUNAWAY ENGINE

We had flown about 15 or 16 missions when we were briefed, on or about April 1, 1945, to bomb a target in Southern Germany. Take-off was uneventful; we proceeded to our gathering place, Buncher 13, some 10 miles south of Great Ashfield. We gained altitude and maneuvered for sometime while getting into our bombing formation. Once this was accomplished, our group slipped into the bomber stream for Germany at altitude.

Sometime after leaving the English coast, our airplane developed a runaway propeller on our #2 engine. It was really wound up and was whining like crazy! The pilots and engineer were frantically trying to get it under control. The pilot realized that if this particular propeller came off it could shear off the nose of the plane with Bill Schloss and me in it! He shouted over our microphone: "get out of the nose!" I grabbed my parachute and a walk-around oxygen bottle. I was making my way back to the radio room, but got stuck in the bomb bay between the two uprights. I tore myself free tearing my life jacket, Mae West, and heated suit. When I got to the radio room I saw our gunners lined up at the back right side door with chutes and ready to bail out. I prepared to join them while plugging in my throat mike and headset so I could hear and talk on the intercom.

The pilot said that our engineer had figured out a way to cut off the fuel supply to the wayward engine and hoped to have it under control in short order, which was accomplished a few minutes later. As the propeller slowed down, the pilot feathered it and our trauma was over. But we were still short one engine! I returned to the nose and took stock of our situation. We were still over the North Sea some distance off the coast and had lost enough altitude so we didn't need oxygen (below 10,000 feet). We made sure there were no British ships or boats beneath us because we knew we couldn't bring our bombs home and had to release them in the North Sea, probably killing a few fish but no Allies!

I was able to navigate us back to Great Ashfield, where we landed no worst for wear, just a little scared! This was our shortest sortie, only about an hour and a half. We didn't get credit for a mission and flew again the next day in a different airplane!

Dough Thanks Airmen
Apr. 25, 1945

To the B-Bag:

I got to thinking that plenty of cracks that we in the infantry make about the Air Force, while seemingly ignored, may be taken more to heart than we think.

I feel that I could never adequately express the feeling that I have toward the Air Force. I believe most infantrymen feel the same way. The Air Force is as necessary to the infantry soldier as the weapon he holds in his hands.

When you are up on the front, and the heavy artillery and mortars come crashing down on you from behind the enemy lines, you have a peculiar feeling in your stomach because you can do nothing about it. It has been the same since D-Day.

But let the rain stop momentarily or a few breaks appear in the clouds. The Air Force needs no more. You see flight after flight of our planes—on their way to return death and destruction to the enemy.

You feel strangely elated. The enemy mortars, the rockets, the artillery have ceased firing. The flak starts mushrooming into life in the sky.

But the planes, as far as the eye can see, are still coming. Your eyes grow moist as you say to yourself, simply— Thank God.—*An Infantry Soldier.*

From Stars and Stripes Armed Forces newspaper.

THE ORDNANCE DEPOT

On April 7, 1945, our group bombed a German Ordnance Depot at Gustrow in Northern Germany. It was some 100 miles northwest of Berlin and near the North Sea. The Luftwaffe came in force to greet us. Two ME-109s and four jets, ME-110s and ME-210s made passes at us. More German jets were watching us from a distance, flying higher than our P-51s liked to fly. Our escort, P-51s, were in there pitching and we lost only one B-17 in a mid-air collision with a ME-109. One ME-109, with a P-51 right on his tail, came through our formation. The P-51 shot him down right in front of us.

We bombed at 15,000 feet visual and had excellent bombing results, blowing the hell out of that installation. One late release overshot the target, but hit an ammunition dump hidden in the woods. Bill Schloss, our bombardier, obviously proud of himself, growled, "Now those Krauts can't tell their arsenals from a hole in the ground!!!"

CZECHOSLOVAKIA MISSIONS

In late April of 1945, the Allies were pushing into Eastern Germany, General George (Old Blood and Guts) Patton and his tanks were sweeping across Southern Germany, and the battle lines were changing daily. The 8th Air Force was having a hard time finding targets in Germany or in the surrounding areas controlled by the Germans. Our last three combat missions were in northern Czechoslovakia to drive out the Germans ahead of Patton.

On April 17 we flew a mission to Ruednice. Our target was an oil storage depot in the woods on the Elbe River, past 14 degrees east longitude. We bombed visual but at our bombing altitude the vapor trails (contrails) were very persistent and we had to fly through a haze from the group ahead of us, but we hit our target right on the nose. There was no flak or bandits in the area. We considered it a long "milk run"!

The next day, April 18, we again flew to Czechoslovakia. We led the 8th Air Force. Our wing commander, General Gerhart, flew in the lead airplane. We were all at our best and flew the best formation we had flown in quite awhile. For most of the trip, we were over friendly territory so we flew at only 2000 feet altitude and were able to see a lot of beautiful country over Belgium, Holland and Germany. There were a lot of beat up towns. The cities had just shells of buildings remaining and the railroads, marshalling yards and bridges were all damaged. We saw Siegfried line up close with all its fortifications, tank traps and battle lines.

Our target was a marshalling yard in Kolin. We blew hell out of it with twelve 500 pound bombs. We had flown up to bombing altitude before we reached the battle lines. Again, there was no flak or bandits in the area. Our luck holds out!

The following day, April 19 we flew to Aussig. We were tail-end Charlie for this mission and things got pretty messed up. We avoided Prague and flew around it; missed our original IP (Initial Point) and had a twenty-four minute bomb run, (eight to ten minutes was average). We hit another marshalling yard and clobbered it. We were flying deputy lead to take over if anything happened to our leader, but we didn't have to.

A number of bandits attacked us with Me 109's, FW-190's and several of the new Jet fighters that the Germans were developing. There were several Me 210s (single-engine) and Me 410s (twin-engine) bandits after us. One Me 210 flew right through our squadron formation from the rear but fortunately, we didn't lose anybody. I could see the pilot's face as he went by. We saw one B 17 go down near Dresden, shot by bandits, and I counted three chutes that got out.

On the way home, we flew over Cologne and saw the whole town leveled except the cathedral which was damaged. The Allies had agreed to leave it as long as the Germans did not use it for an observation post. There were five bridges down on the Rhine there. Only pontoon bridges, built by our engineers, remained. This was our crew's last real combat mission in the war.

THANK THE LORD AND ALL HIS ANGELS!!!

BIG 24   April 17, 1945

To: RUEDNICE -- Czechoslovakia

With Fauber and crew in "Queenie".

     Helping Patton -- bombed visual but contrails all over the place made things hazy --bombed an oil storage depot in the woods on Elbe River -- clobbered it, too!

     Had a Bombardier today -- Olsen-- a new boy but good -- flew in deputy lead -- to take over on bomb run in case -- so had to be on that old pelote all the way in.

     Salvoed 6 - 1000# bombs.

     Saw Patton's front lines where they took Hof and saw about 10 little towns on fire along lines--

     Target was past 14 degrees east!!

     0830 hrs. in air, long haul for these days. No flak, no fighters -- long milk run! Tactical Air Force Now!!

(27)

BIG 25 April 18, 1945

To: <u>KOLIN</u> -- Czechoslovakia

With Fauber (1st. Lt. today!) and crew.

    Another long haul -- 0930 hrs. in air.

    Helping Patton <u>and</u> the Russians today.

    Hit marshalling yard with 12 -- 500#
bombs. Blew the Hell out of it -- we had to,
we had General Gerhart in lead ship!!
Best Fo-mation we've flown for quite awhile!
Flew over Belgium, Holland and Germany at
2000' buzzing the troops for morale purposes,
I guess -- really saw a lot of beautiful
country -- saw a lot of beat up towns, too --
saw Siegfried line with all the tank traps
and battle lines later. Took Lunch!!

(28)

BIG 26   April 19, 1945

To: <u>AUSSIG</u> -- Czechoslavakia again!

With Fauber and crew in "Queenie"

    Pilot flew as Co-pilot -- MacCrussen,
Major "Moon" Mullins led today and we were
tail end Charlie so things were a bit screwed
up.

    Missed I.P. and flew around Prague --
then had 24 minute bomb run -- with bandits
in the area, too! Jets!

    Hit marshalling yard with 14 - 250#
bombs and 4 - 500# incendiaries. Clobbered
it!!

    Flew #2 again so Bill and I had to get
up for lead crew briefing.

    Saw one B-17 go down in spin by Dresden -
shot by fighters -- 3 chutes got out!!

    0900 hours in air. No Flak!!

    Flew over Cologne and the whole town
is level except the cathedral and it has a
few holes in it!! 5 bridges down there!!

(29)

FOOD DROP MISSIONS
APRIL AND MAY, 1945
GERMAN-OCCUPIED HOLLAND

The war in Europe was winding down. Gen. George (Old Blood and Guts) Patton and his tanks were sweeping across Southern Germany. They were going so fast that one mission we were scheduled to fly to bomb towns just ahead of Patton was scrubbed after we were in the air because his troops had already taken the targeted towns. Monty Montgomery, Omar Bradley and General Patch were closing in on Berlin.

The 8th Air Force was running out of targets. Our crew's last three combat missions were to Czechoslovakia! On each mission we were over 10 hours in the air and took our lunches. We saw a lot of beautiful country as well as beat-up cities and towns, both coming and going. The targets weren't easy; there was plenty of flak and a few Luftwaffe fighters in the area. We saw several new jet planes. We had done our job and the ground forces and tactical air force were still slugging it out with the enemy.

General Jimmie Doolittle was the Commander of the 8th Air Force based in England. Word came to the Allies that the Dutch people, who had been conquered and occupied for more than five years, were starving to death. The Germans, in Holland, had been by-passed by the Allied Forces, thereby cutting them off from their supplies. There was very little food for them, let alone any food for the Dutch. A month or so before the end of the war, Queen Wilhelmina of the Netherlands, ordered her people to strike passively and not cooperate with their German captors. The Germans retaliated by breaking the levees and dams, and flooding the fields so that the Dutch had no way of raising food.

A deal was made with the German High Command for the Americans and British to bring food to the Dutch people by air. The Americans would use B-17 heavy bombers and the British Lancasters and Sterlings. Corridors were set up. As long as our airplanes stayed in those corridors both coming and going, the Germans on the ground had orders not to shoot at us. The British named their operation "Manna" from the Bible "Food from Heaven." Their crews called it "Biscuit Bombing." The Americans, not so creative, designated it as "Operation Chowhound." Our crews called it "Doolittle's Delicatessen" or "Spam Runs." Our crew, 1st Lt. Clarence Fauber's, flew four of these food-drop missions. I was the navigator. We were part of the 549th Squadron, 385th Bomb Group (heavy), 3rd Wing of the 8th Air Force based out of Great Ashfield, Suffolk, England. The plan was to put the food: 10-0-1 rations, cheeses, meats, canned foods, etc. into heavy canvas bags and drop them "free-fall" into the fields. Each B-17 would fly as a single ship, not in formation. Over 3 tons (6000 lbs.) of food would be carried by each plane per trip. We would drop the food from about 200 feet altitude at almost stalling speed, about 100 mph.

On our first food-drop mission on April 30, 1945 (as I recall), I flew with a new replacement crew as the bombardier. I thought this would be great: I could sit up in the plexiglas nose, relax, enjoy the scenery, drop the food in the designated area and come home happy. I didn't realize it at the time, but the young navigator had no clue how to find our corridor and the rest of the crew was just as green!

I was enjoying the views of the little towns, fields, and even people on the ground. They waved to us. We could see German troops, flak towers and fortifications everywhere. I suddenly realized that we were flying over a city and were several miles to the left of our corridor. I had been promoted to 1st Lieutenant the week before and I became aware that the other three officers were 2nd Lts. which made me the ranking officer on board. I had never been ranking anything before in my life! I took over command of the airplane for the remainder of the mission. We were "Fair Game" for the German gunners! I immediately took over the navigation and told the pilot to head for the open sea at full speed and pray! The city below us was Amsterdam. The closer we got to the North Sea, the more Germans, flak towers, guns, etc., we could see on the ground. Apparently the Germans were as surprised to see us as we were them and they didn't shoot at us or if they did, they didn't hit us. We made our way out to the North Sea at about 250 mph, made a big U-turn and came back into our corridor. At the last minute, I got into the bombardier's chair, opened the bomb bay and salvoed our load of food into one of the designated fields. I really appreciated my regular crew from then on!

My second food-drop mission, and the first with our entire crew was on May 2. I went back to my regular job of navigator. Some sorehead Germans shot at us with their 20mm cannons, damaging several planes in our group, but not bringing down any. Because of this, all of the group's crew members that participated got credit for a combat mission. This was our pilot's 24th mission and my 27th. A selected number of the groups' officers were awarded medals from the Dutch Government for this mission. None of our crew got any medals or any other special recognition from the Dutch or anyone else. Our Squadron Commander, Colonel Charles Reid and Captain Randall, his deputy, felt that this was part of our job, something that had to be done therefore, there was nothing special to be recognized. I did not know if any of the 549th bomb squadron received any medals or any recognition.

On our third mission on May 4, we had a couple of crew chiefs fly with us. Normally, they were "ground pounders" and were not expected to fly, but they wanted to fly a "mission" before the war ended. This mission was uneventful; we hit our corridor right on the button. We dropped our food in an open field and then toured quite a bit of Holland. We pointed things out to the crew chiefs before returning home without trouble. However, one sack of food got hung up in the bomb bay and our bombardier tried to kick it out, but to no avail. We brought it back with us, sneaked it out of the plane, took it to our barracks and enjoyed the food!

Our fourth and last food-drop mission was on May 7. While we were in the air, word came that Germany had capitulated and the war in Europe was over!! The next day, May 8 was officially declared V-E Day (victory in Europe). Apparently the Dutch people had gotten the news also, because we could see wild demonstrations on the ground everywhere we went. We could plainly see the happy faces of the people. There were thousands of Dutch flags flying and an American flag here and there. One fellow waved his long-handled underwear at us. We saw a young girl get knocked off of her bicycle by the prop-wash from the plane just ahead of us. Some Germans shot at us. Our plane was hit in the wing by small arms fire. We could see a hole about 8 inches across in the top of our wing. Apparently, a 9mm rifle or machine gun bullet went through the wing, hitting a wing spar. The entry hole on the bottom of the wing was 9mm but the exit hole was 8 to 10 inches across. This was major battle damage to our plane, rendering it incapable of flying the next mission.

Our airplane received the last combat damage in the 8th Air Force in World War II and our crew got credit for the last mission flown. For this mission, we had volunteers all over the place to fly with us. These were crew chiefs, mechanics, office personnel and even a few doctors who, as "ground pounders" never flew. I guess they wanted to tell their grandchildren how they had flown a combat mission over enemy territory! We had a number of them in our plane for this mission. Bill Schloss and I had three "observers" in the nose with us.

The 8th Air Force flew some 1430 sorties and dropped 4,300 tons of food in the operation. The British dropped another 6,000 tons of food. With our four missions, our crew delivered some 25,000 pounds (twelve and a half tons) of food to Holand! When hostilities ended, ships could come into the ports and the air food-drops were no longer needed. We were most happy to have participated in this worthy cause, hopefully having saved many lives from starvation.

On our first food-drop mission, as a crew, we pooled our candy, Hershey's Milk Chocolate bars and gum allotments and put them into a red waterproof bag supplied by our co-pilot, and dropped it for the children along with the sacks of food. On the next mission, our entire barracks contributed all the candy we could get our hands on for our crew to drop. Our crew became known around the squadron as "Fauber's Candy Bombers."

Fifty four years later, these missions took on a strange quirk of fate and coincidence. These were paths that were meant to be and meant to cross! My wife, Mary Esther, and I were at a dinner party in a friend's home here in our hometown of Tucson, Arizona.

Our hosts were a Dutch couple who had worked and traveled all over the world before retiring in Tucson. During a conversation, the food-drop was mentioned and my wife interjected that I had dropped food into Holland at the end of the war. Our hostess, with tears in her eyes, said, "I was one of the Dutch people that saw the planes and received the food. Our family was reduced to digging for bulbs and eating them to survive. We loved the Americans for saving our lives." At that point in the conversation both my wife and our hostess were near tears; they hugged and knew that they had to change the subject. Her husband said that he also was there, saw the planes and got the food. They were teenagers at the time and recalled the food-drop operation vividly from the receiving end. Needless to say, we have become very good friends. How paths cross and bonds are formed!

U.S. Army Air Force Photos

MANNA FROM HEAVEN FOR THE DUTCH:
Crews of the 8th Air Force, accustomed to high altitude bombing, skimmed in low over Dutch cities to drop hundreds of cases of ten-in-one rations to the beleaguered civilian population. These pictures show a 385th Bomb Group Fort dropping its "mercy cargo." On each of the first three days of May approximately 400 B17s sent 800 tons of food down toward areas carefully marked off by the Dutch and just as carefully pin-pointed by the airmen.

From Stars and Stripes Armed Forces newspaper of May 7, 1945.

BIG 27

May 7, 1945

V.E. DAY!!
"Spam Run"

To: AMSTERDAM -- "of all places"

With Fauber and crew in "Queenie"

Last mission flown by the 8th. Air Force
in E.T.O.!

"Doolittles Delicatessen" taking
10-0-1 rations and food into Holland to
keep the Dutchmen alive -- dropped 75 - **80**^{tt}
sacks of food on airfield at 400 ft.
altitude -- buzzed Amsterdam, Rotterdam,
the Hague, and half of Holland -- knocked a
gal off her bike with prop wash -- 100s
of Dutch flags out everywhere-- one joker
was even waving his long-handled drawers
at us -- saw a bunch of Krauts at fortifications along North Sea Coast -- waved to
them -- they even waved back -- some sorehead took a shot at us and we came home with
a big hole in our wing -- major battle
damage!!

Saw some flak towers at close range --
almost tempted to drop a grenade on them
but held my fire -- lots of guts, but no
grenades!! More legal buzzing I've never
seen.

Went over in single ships so had to do
lots of navigating!!

Operation - "Chowhound"
My fourth food drop but the
only one that counted - no one was
hit on the others. (30) *May 1, 3, 5, 7*

ADDENDUM TO FOOD DROP MISSIONS

After writing my memories of the Food Drop Mission I read our co-pilot's diary. He mentioned that when we flew over Holland, he remembered the big signs in the fields. They spelled out "THANK YOU" with big rocks so that we could see them plainly in the drop areas. I recalled this vividly and remembered thinking that these people were really appreciative of our efforts to bring them food.

Our missions were somewhat dangerous in that the Germans on the ground could have failed to receive the orders to not shoot at us, or they could have disregarded them and shot at us anyway. Flying low and slow made us an easy, vulnerable target for them. Flying at almost a stalling speed was a hazard in any circumstance. A wind gust could easily have sent us tumbling.

We all felt good about helping the Dutch people in their hour of need and always returned home with a feeling of pride and great satisfaction that we may have saved the lives of many innocents.

Many years later, a Bombardier friend of mine was on a tour of Europe when he fell and broke his arm while touring Holland. He went to a Dutch hospital for treatment and the doctors set his arm, put it in a cast and kept him in the hospital for a couple of days. When the hospital staff learned that he had participated in the food drop missions, they waived all charges for their services.

I learned about "Liberation Bread" in 1945 in Holland. We were called the "Eagles of Mercy" for our part in the operation. We had helped ease the ravages of the "Hunger Winter."

Part of our delivery of food was flour, sugar, butter, as well as Canadian and American wheat. The Dutch bakers used this to make a white bread, which for many in the starving country, tasted like cake! They called it "Liberation Bread."

From time to time since then, bakers made this bread for sale. In 2005 the year's remake was made of special wheat flour, butter and sugar, making the bread taste mildly sweet as before. The top of each loaf had an imprint of a B-17 bomber on it! Some 2700 bakeries all over the country were asked to participate in this project.

In commemoration of the air drops, the Dutch had a fly-over by many planes such as the Dutch Royal Air Force, as well as the American and British Air Forces. At a number of areas of the country, one of the planes made a low level fly-over and dropped a load of "Liberation Bread." The Dutch people relived the Manna and Chowhound Missions by the British and American 8th Air Force.

All of us that had participated in this operation were happy for the Dutch and proud to have been a part of it.

THANK YOU
BOYS.

57425 A.C.

UNCENSORED   War Theatre #12 (Holland) MISCELLANEOUS   (over)

A Thank You sign in a field done in chalk by the Dutch during the Food Drop Operation.

New York — London Edition — Paris

VE-DAY

THE STARS AND STRIPES

Daily Newspaper of U.S. Armed Forces — in the European Theater of Operations
Vol. 5 No. 158—1d. TUESDAY, MAY 8, 1945 ★

VE-DAY

GERMANY QUITS

Today, May 8, is VE-Day, and will be officially proclaimed so by the leaders of the Big Three in simultaneous declarations in Washington, London and Moscow.

This was announced last night following unofficial celebrations yesterday afternoon throughout the world, inspired by a broadcast by Germany's new Foreign Minister that the Wehrmacht High Command had ordered its armed forces to surrender unconditionally, and by press reports, unconfirmed by SHAEF, that the Reich's capitulation to the Allies and Soviets had been signed early yesterday morning at Rheims, France, at a schoolhouse serving as Gen. Eisenhower's HQ.

U.S. Really Let Go With Yells At (Unofficial) Peace News

NEW YORK, May 7—Clouds of torn paper and ticker tape swirled down on screaming crowds packed in the streets of New York this morning within a few minutes after news had been received that Germany had surrendered unconditionally.

Office girls opened windows and emptied wastebaskets. Bits of paper fluttered in clouds all over Manhattan and settled in a thick carpet on the damp streets.

Some offices closed as soon as word was received from Associated Press at 9:35 AM and employes joined the thousands milling through the thoroughfares.

City authorities said the crowds, estimated at 1,000,000 persons, were "bigger than 1918." The streets were knee deep in paper, all phones were dead and traffic was diverted.

In the Hudson River liners and tugs let loose their sirens, adding to the noise of planes that dipped crazily over the city. The whole city was gripped by the spirit of celebration.

In Times Square cheers rang out and couples danced through a blizzard of confetti. Service men of many nations mingled in the packed victory throng.

Outside one Broadway hotel, a group of Americans, British and Canadian servicemen formed a grinning line, while a long string of girls marched past placing congratulatory kisses on their lipstick-covered faces.

In the financial district, coatless and hatless men and women filled the narrow streets, their yells accompanied by the ceaseless honking of automobile horns.

New York newspapers rushed out with extras based on the AP dispatch. The Journal-American carried a banner in type three and one-half inches deep "It's VE-Day." The Sun had a two-line banner (Continued on page 3)

London Shouts 'It's All Over'

News of Germany's final capitulation yesterday hit streets jammed with thousands of Londoners—and Americans—milling around in excited groups, cramming sidewalks until they flowed over into the streets, still awaiting the official word on the surrender but satisfied that the Hun had quit.

Whitehall crowds reached Times Square proportions as expectant mobs stopped nearly all sidewalk traffic in an effort to get close to the Ministry of Health building where Prime Minister Churchill was expected to speak from a flag-decked balcony. Eventually, they rolled out onto the street and traffic there came to a standstill, except for a beer truck which clattered down the street, draped with Aussies singing Tipperary at the tops of their voices.

Even the bobbies were not their unruffled selves, as they shrugged their shoulders, doffed their hats and mopped their brows after attempting to handle the growing mobs. One even got mixed up trying to give a GI directions to Piccadilly.

Piccadilly, of course, was packed—mostly with GIs—and dominated by a carnival spirit, with all the hurdy- (Continued on page 3)

THEY SIGNED: Associated Press reported that among those who signed the terms by which Germany surrendered unconditionally to the Allies were Lt. Gen. Walter B. Smith, Gen. Eisenhower's chief of staff (left), and Col. Gen. Gustav Jodl, the Wehrmacht's new chief of staff.

Passes, Furloughs Extended 48 Hours

Effective with the official announcement of VE-Day today, passes and furloughs of all military personnel in the U.K. are extended for 48 hours, U.K. Base AG announced yesterday.

Neutral Swiss Rejoice

BERN, May 7—All church bells in Switzerland were rung for a quarter of an hour following news of the unconditional surrender by the Germans. And although there was no planned victory celebration, the neutral Swiss, who never made any secret of their Allied sympathies, greeted the end of the war in Europe with cheers and rejoicing.

Following publication yesterday afternoon of an Associated Press dispatch datelined Rheims and reporting that the surrender terms were signed by Lt. Gen. Walter Bedell Smith, Gen. Eisenhower's chief of staff; Russian Gen. Ivan A. Suslapatov and French Gen. Francois Sevez, for the Allies and Russia, and Col. Gen. Gustav Jodl, new Wehrmacht chief of staff, for the Germans, the British Ministry of Information announced in London that today would be treated as VE-Day, ending the war five years, eight months and seven days after the Nazis invaded Poland on Sept. 1, 1939.

Prime Minister Churchill will broadcast the proclamation to the British at 3 PM in London today. Since the announcement will be made simultaneously by the Big Three leaders, this means that the statements by President Truman and Marshal Stalin will be broadcast from Washington and Moscow at 9 AM and 4 PM respectively.

Breaking by The Associated Press of the story on the surrender negotiations created a furore, coming soon after Flensburg Radio, on the Danish-German border, carried the broadcast announcing Germany's unconditional surrender.

SHAEF authorized correspondents there to state that, as of 4:45 PM yesterday, it had not made anywhere any official statement for publication up to that hour concerning the complete surrender of all the German armed forces in Europe, and that no story to that effect had been authorized. United Press and International News Service said dispatches from their Paris bureaus told of the suspension by Allied military authorities of the Associated Press filing of news dispatches from the ETO because of its Rheims dispatch.

Lack of direct confirmation for the Rheims story—though there was no outright denial of the details—created considerable confusion before the Ministry of Information announcement was released. The Columbia Broadcasting System's chief correspondent in London reported in a broadcast to New York that both Truman and Churchill were prepared to issue their proclamation last night, but that Marshal Stalin was not ready to do so, with the result that all three had agreed to postpone the announcements until they could be made at the same time.

In Washington yesterday afternoon President Truman announced, through his press secretary Jonathan Daniels, that he had agreed with London and (Continued on back page)

Stars and Stripes Armed Forces newspaper on V-E Day, May 8, 1945.

V-E DAY

On our last Food Drop Mission on May 7, while we were in the air, we heard that Germany had capitulated and the war was over. We all cheered and were ecstatic on the way home. We had lived through the war and would be going home to the "good, old U.S. of A." When we landed we found our base in celebration! We immediately joined in with the shooting of our guns into the air and congratulating each other for being "still alive in Forty Five."

The celebrating went on into the night. The bars in the Officers' and NCOs Clubs had no closing time as they did usually. The bars closed early when a mission was planned for the next day. This was different; it was a time for great jubilation, so we all drank, sang and acted crazy. I had my first real drink with my pilot, Clarence. The entire base went "NUTS"! As it got dark, we shot flares into the air from our Verey pistols. That continued into the night. It was like watching the Fourth of July fireworks.

The next day, which was declared V-E Day, (Victory in Europe), the celebrations continued but they were not as wild as the night before. Everyone was trying to send a message home telling the homefolks and loved ones that we would be home soon. No longer would our letters and messages be censored! I sent my Mom a cablegram that said, "Start baking pies Mom, I'll be home soon!"

Our commander, Colonel Jumper, called the entire group together on the tarmac, surrounded by our planes, to say "thanks" for a job well done and to go home to a safe and happy life!

We all felt that we had won the war and that we were
IN LIKE FLYNN !!!

How Our Cartoonists See It

HUBERT by SGT. DICK WINGERT

"Holy Smoke! At 11.1 o'clo—Hey soldier, you stop that! D'ya hear?"

UP FRONT WITH MAULDIN

"To hell with it . . . I ain't standin' up till he does."

PRIVATE BREGER

Germany Collapsed as Her Waterlines Fell

Over the Rivers—to Victory

By William E. Taylor
Stars and Stripes Staff Writer

Breaching of Germany's mighty river defenses on three major fronts—the Rhine on the west, the Oder in the east and the Po in the south—opened the final battle that crushed the Third Reich and routed the Wehrmacht and its last-minute rag-tag Volkssturm partner into laying down arms by the millions.

Once their last natural defense lines were destroyed the Germans crumbled quickly. The Rhine was stormed in force on Mar. 25 and little more than a month later the Reich was split by the American-Soviet juncture at Torgau, on the Elbe. Crossing of the Elbe east of Berlin by the Russians and the Allied campaign in Italy both began in mid-April, and the Reich capital and the enemy armies in Italy quit the fight on May 2.

It had taken both lives and time for the forces against Germany to mass on the Rhine, Oder and Po. Behind the Allies in the west lay the broken remains of the Atlantic Wall, the Siegfried Line and the Roer and Saar bastions; in Italy, Monte Cassino was the symbol of the hard fight northward through the rugged, many-rivered and mountainous peninsula. Pushing west on the long front from Leningrad southward to Stalingrad, farthest point reached by the Nazis, the Red Army had hurdled the Don, Dnieper, Berezina, Bug, Dniester and Vistula rivers.

Reds Take Offensive

In mid-January the Russians went over to the offensive on a 600-mile front from East Prussia southward to Czechoslovakia, stormed the Vistula, captured Warsaw and Cracow and began the battle for Budapest. Within a week the Red Army, in one of its characteristic sweeps, covered half the distance from its starting point to Berlin. Silesia's industrial area, which served with the Ruhr and Saar, in the west, to keep the Reich's war machine running, came under attack as the Soviets reached the Oder in the Breslau area.

About that time the Allies were recovering from the enemy counter-offensive in the icy, snow-bound Ardennes—the Wehrmacht's last major concerted blow. Although it failed, the enemy thrust into Belgium and Luxemburg cost the Allies 40,000 casualties, split the 12th Army Group temporarily and changed the groupings farther south when the 3rd Army, then along the Saar River, was moved northward and sent into the attack on the southern part of the bulge. Companion counter-drives by the Germans in the Saar-Palatinate's southern edge forced the 7th Army to abandon its then meager holdings in Germany and to withdraw southward into Alsace-Lorraine.

The Soviets were in Pomerania late in January. On the west, American troops had already breached the Siegfried Line in the Aachen area, were pressing on the Roer River in the northern sector and were preparing to batter down the enemy line farther south.

Closer Liaison Announced

On Feb. 12 the results of the Big Three talks at Yalta were announced. Primary point in the list of accomplishments in the military field was the disclosure of the closest possible liaison between the Allied Supreme Command and the Red Army high command in their joint operations for defeating Germany.

With the winning of the Roer dams, one of which the enemy blew and held up the Americans for a time, the way was cleared for a push across this river and on to the Rhine. Feb. 23 saw both the 1st and 9th Armies across the Roer; it was no picnic, for the Germans fought hard. But when the enemy finally broke the Allied campaign gathered momentum and never lost it until the Elbe was reached and crossed in fulfilment of Allied plans for meeting with the Soviets in the heart of the Third Reich.

Budapest fell on Feb. 13. The long siege for Hungary's capital and their futile efforts to break the Soviet ring around the city had cost the Germans 100,000 men.

Gen. Eisenhower set his troops the task of destroying the German Army west of the Rhine. On Mar. 2 the 9th Army reached the Rhine, first U.S. force to do so, and was quickly followed by 1st Army surges to the river at points to the south.

Bridges Crump into Rhine

Bridge after bridge crumpled into the Rhine as the enemy blasted the arteries through which the Allies could hurdle the barrier into the central Reich.

Then came one of the Allies' most fortunate flukes of the war, a break won by courage and initiative—the seizure intact of the Ludendorf bridge across the Rhine at Remagen on Mar. 7, putting the Americans across the river even as armchair strategists were speculating on how long it would take to crush the enemy line.

In mid-March, while 8th Air Force planes hit German HQ near Berlin, the 3rd and 7th Armies opened simultaneous operations to crush the Saar-Palatinate and clear the Germans from this industrial zone. The 7th, after its push through France, clearing Alsace and the Rhine south of the Saar district, struck into the southern edge of the roughly shaped Saar triangle, battering down Siegfried defenses along the border.

The 3rd Army, moving on a wide front from the Moselle to the southeast—in the manner of an alligator jaw clamping shut—sent tanks roaring into the enemy's rear zones for a link-up with the 7th Army. Two German armies were shattered in the combined attack, which brought the Americans to the Rhine on another long stretch and gave the Allies control over virtually all of the western bank of the river from north to south.

While the Soviets were fighting in Silesia in the south and for the Baltic ports of Gdynia, Danzig and Stettin in the north, the Germans looked for further heavy blows by the Allies, focusing attention on the northern sectors of the Rhine, where the British had cloaked their operations under the war's greatest smokescreen.

And while the Germans were thus absorbed in the north the 3rd Army went across the Rhine to the south and shook the 4th Armored Division loose in one of the most spectacular armored rampages of any campaign.

Airborne Descend in North

On Mar. 25, two days after the 3rd Army's crossing, Allied paratroops and airborne infantry descended upon the Germans in the north as the British and Americans stormed the Rhine in the Wesel area. A day later the 7th Army was over the river, crossing south of the 3rd Army's sector.

Germany lost Gdynia to the Soviets on Mar. 28; Danzig fell two days later.

By Apr. 1 the 1st and 9th Armies had sealed off the Ruhr, trapping enemy forces later found to number more than 300,000, as the 9th slashed eastward from its Rhine bridgeheads and linked up with 1st Army forces fanning out from the Remagen bridgehead.

"Security silence" became a byword covering Allied operations east of the Rhine. There was no point in telling the Germans what the disorganization of their armies prevented them from knowing. So all the world waited to find out what went on.

Meanwhile, the Soviets continued to build up their striking forces all along the Oder in preparation for the final campaign of the war. Wiener-Neustadt, Austrian plane production center, and Bratislava, key to Vienna, were captured Apr. 3 and 4 respectively. In the north, Konigsberg, East Prussian capital, fell Apr. 10.

Then the curtain lifted on Allied operations to show the 9th Army on the Elbe. A day later, Apr. 12, the Americans were over the river at a point about 60 miles southwest of Berlin. There was talk of a race between the Americans and Soviets as to who would reach the Reich capital first. Not until later did it become apparent that the Elbe was to serve as the limit of the Allied thrusts eastward into Germany and Russian drives westward.

Germany's chief seaports on the North Sea and unconquered areas of Holland were under assault by the British 2nd and Canadian 1st Armies as all along the rest of the front the Americans drove for a link-up with the Soviets, who captured Vienna, capital of Austria, on Apr. 13.

Smash Out in Italy

In Italy the U.S. 5th and British 8th Armies struck in mid-April. As they breached the Po River and sent columns speeding into the disorganized enemy areas the Italian partisans in the principal cities in the north rose in revolt and seized power. Mussolini was captured and summarily executed on Apr. 28.

In less than three weeks' time the Germans and Fascists were finished in Italy. Unconditional surrender of nearly 1,000,000 troops in northern Italy and in parts of five Austrian provinces was announced May 2.

Even as the Allies struck in Italy the Russians stormed the Oder east of Berlin, finally confirming the many reports put out by the Nazis of such a thrust toward the German capital.

One by one Germany's great cities had fallen. Now it was Berlin's turn. The garrison laid down arms on May 2, and the German radio, building up the Hitler legend to its apex, said that Hitler had died in defense of the capital. But the failure of Soviet troops to find the Fuehrer's body in the rubble of Berlin's Chancellery, where the Nazis said he perished, only served to heighten the skepticism concerning Hitler's finish. Apparently he was dead, but how and where remained a mystery.

1st Army 1st Again

There was no cohesive enemy front left in the Reich after the 1st Army troops—first to enter Germany, first to capture a Reich city (Aachen), first across the Rhine—became the first Americans to link up with the Red Army, at Torgau, on the Elbe, on Apr. 26. The Reich was cut in two.

Germany's redoubt had been under assault by the U.S. 3rd and 7th and French 1st Armies. Touted as the Nazis' last-ditch stand, it turned out to be another Nazi lie. Berchtesgaden's capture came soon after the fall of Nuremberg and Munich—and the latter city, Nazism's birthplace, turned out to be the scene of the first concrete anti-Nazi group so far discovered in Germany.

New junctures between the Allies and Russians along the Elbe squeezed the Germans tighter in the north. The enemy fled from the Soviet advance and gave up to the Allies. The enemy quit on May 5 in northwest Germany, Holland and Denmark, giving up to the 21st Army Group, which found itself swamped under hordes of panicky German troops and civilians.

Following the Nazi line to the end, Grand Adm. Karl Doenitz, who proclaimed himself the beaten Reich's new leader, sought to split the Anglo-American-Russian front by saying the Germans didn't want to fight except against the Soviet Union. What he said affected the military situation in no way, however. The Wehrmacht was beaten, its commanders streamed in to give themselves up. Nazi leaders had gone underground, some of them literally, perhaps.

Defeat Will Really Cut 'Em Down

Fourth Reich Will Be a Smaller, Quieter Place

By Sigrid Arne
Associated Press Writer

NEW YORK, May 7 (AP)—Germany faces a much shrunken future, both in acreage and in bombast.

To the east she will lose a large stretch of territory to Poland. At the Yalta Conference the late President Roosevelt, Prime Minister Churchill and Marshal Stalin recognized that Poland must receive substantial accessions of territory in the north and west.

Later Churchill told the House of Commons that Poland would receive most of East Prussia, Danzig and Upper Silesia. These areas include valuable coal deposits and much industrial strength.

Churchill said further that he favored a "shifting of population" if necessary—meaning that Germans in these areas may be moved back into what is left of Germany. The Russian grapevine has said that Stalin also approves the idea.

The Netherlands Government has announced that it "reserves the right to claim compensation," but that nothing can be done until the Dutch people are free to "express their will." How much territory that means is not known, but at this point the farm lands of western Holland are flooded. Some 5,000,000 Dutch farmers lived in this region.

Deputy Prime Minister Clement R. Attlee told the House of Commons recently that the British backed the Dutch viewpoint.

All along the old western frontier France may demand considerable territory. Gen. Charles de Gaulle told a recent press conference in Paris that "France does not want to see the end of the war without her forces permanently stationed from one end of the Rhine to the other."

Includes Ruhr's Might

This would include the steel cities in the Saar basin and much of the Ruhr's industrial might.

But all this remains to be delineated in an Allied conference which will both draw the new borders and set the reparations to be demanded of Germany.

A Big Three commission is now sitting in Moscow and working out these questions of reparation. Reparations "in kind" mean, of course, food, raw materials and manufactured goods—what ever Germany can produce in excess of her minimum needs.

There can be no adequate prophecy how long Germany will be occupied by American, British, Russian and French troops. But for some time to come their chiefs of staff will sit in Berlin to iron out uniform policies for the revolution which the Allies are determined must come in German thinking and living habits.

Their most complicated jobs will be the liquidation of the German war machine—both military and industrial—which was promised at Yalta. Some of Germany's industry will either be destroyed or the machines will be moved to her devastated neighbors.

Will Continue to Work

Some industry—the kind that can turn out peace-time goods, will continue to work, but under Allied control, both to manufacture goods for reparations to other countries and to supply Germany's needs.

Germany's shrunken bombast will disappear when the military are stripped of their uniforms for good. It was decided at Yalta that the Allies would "break up for all time the German General Staff," and "wipe out the National Socialist party."

A large number of Germans will be rounded up for shipment to the countries they wrecked. There they will stand trial for their war crimes.

The United Nations' Relief and Rehabilitation Administration charter says that relief supplies will go only to Allied nationals, or to German citizens who were persecuted for political or religious beliefs—most of them Jews.

The unofficial view in Washington is that as Germany fed herself throughout the war, she can manage in the peace. If, on the other hand, she has more food than she needs, her excess stocks will be apportioned among her victims.

THE STARS AND STRIPES

Printed at The Times Publishing Company, Ltd., for U.S. Armed forces, under auspices of The Information and Education Division, ETOUSA.

Contents passed by the U.S. Army and Navy censors; subscription 26 shillings per year plus postage. ETO edition. Entered as second class matter Mar. 15, 1943, at the post office, New York, N.Y., under the Act of Mar. 3, 1879. All material appearing in this publication has been written and edited by uniformed members of the Army and Navy except where stated that a civilian or other outside source is being quoted.

Editorial and Business office—The Times, Printing House Sq., London, EC4 (Tel. Cen. 2000). District Offices: Bedford 2184; Swindon 3424; Sutton Coldfield.—Four Oaks 268.

Vol. 5, No. 158, May 8, 1945

Stars and Stripes Armed Forces newspaper on V-E Day, May 8, 1945.

DUNKERQUE (DUNKIRK)

The small port and community of Dunkerque, France is on the coast just across the English Channel from Dover, where the famous White Cliffs are. It became famous when the British and their Allies evacuated mainland Europe early in World War II to escape Hitler's relentless German army.

This was an historic evacuation. Every British warship, troop ship, fishing boat, pleasure boat and even some rowboats participated. This was a national operation and everybody participated eagerly. The entire Allied force was able to get out of France on time.

Later in the war, the Allies returned to France with the D-Day landings. These were on the beaches west of Dunkerque. The town and port were heavily fortified by the Germans. The Allies tried to take it while they were liberating France from the German Occupation. It turned out to be too formidable, so our armies by passed it, leaving it cut off from the German Army. It remained occupied by Germans for the remainder of the war.

The Germans at Dunkerque had a large number of 88mm Flak guns, smaller anti-aircraft guns, machine guns and rifles. They seemed to have an endless supply of ammunition for all of them. Our air forces skirted this fortress whenever possible when flying to and from missions over France and Germany.

ESCAPE KITS

In the event that we were shot down, parachuted out or crashed in enemy territory and were not immediately captured, we each carried a small escape kit. It was in a sealed container about seven inches long, five inches wide and one and a quarter inches deep and put in a brown canvas packet. It fit nicely in a pocket of our flight suits just below the knee so that we would always have it with us.

As I recall, each kit contained maps of Western Europe made of silk that were very thin but strong and waterproof. Other items were a small compass, a small knife and a number of squares of high protein candy wrapped in wax paper. There were other items but I don't remember what they were.

We also carried two pictures of ourselves in civilian clothes to resemble Frenchmen, in case we were lucky enough to find the French underground. With the pictures, the French could make us papers that could help us get to the Spanish border and to freedom. The pictures were taken of us at Great Ashfield, using false front suits and ties on a board that we held up in front of us while they took our pictures.

In looking over my pictures, I found that I had ended up with a picture of each of our crew. Unbeknownst to me then, the time would come that I would use those pictures to commemorate their heroism and friendship almost 70 years later.

Fortunately, our crew flew all round-trip missions and none of us needed to use our escape kits.

ESCAPE PICTURES

Fauber Smeltzer Schaefer

Schloss   Elder   Donnelly

DeMucci   Hake   Hatch

FLAK!

Recently, I was showing my grandson around the Pima Air and Space Museum in Tucson, Arizona. While we were in the hangar with the B-17 "I'll Be Around", he asked me, "Papa, what is flak, I thought it was just puffs of smoke?" I immediately explained it this way. The word Flak comes from the German name for anti-aircraft guns. The F is for "Fleger", meaning Airplane and the K is for Kannon meaning "big gun." I don't know what the L or the A mean, but I will try to find out.

The most numerous and popular of those Flak guns were the 88mm. (about 3½ inches in diameter). The entire shell was about 30 inches in length with a projectile that was about 7 inches long and weighed in the vicinity of ten to twelve pounds. These had explosive devices inside that were preset for an exact altitude. When this device detonated, the projectile exploded into hundreds of jagged pieces of shrapnel that could tear an airplane apart and kill or wound its occupants. The explosive that detonated these projectiles produced big puffs of smoke. The 88mm Flak guns made black smoke; the 105mm and 155mm guns produced white smoke. Bright, red flashes could be seen in close bursts. Many times our plane was rocked by these explosives but fortunately, none were lethal. A number of our B-17s were shot down and almost all came home with various amounts of Flak damage.

The overused phrase "twelve o'clock high" usually referred to bandits (enemy aircraft) coming at our airplane directly in front of us at a high angle. But, what ran chills through us the bomber crews, was the Bombardier's announcement of "Flak twelve o'clock level" because we knew we were flying right into it and the German gunners had our speed and altitude zeroed in, which sent an ominous and chilling feeling through all of us.

In 1945, when our crew flew our missions, the Allies had "air superiority" and we only saw bandits sporadically. The P51s carried wing tanks of gasoline so they could escort us all the way, protecting us. Most of the time, Flak was the greatest hazard on our missions.

Flak over Berlin. Photos by Bob Hake, tail gunner.

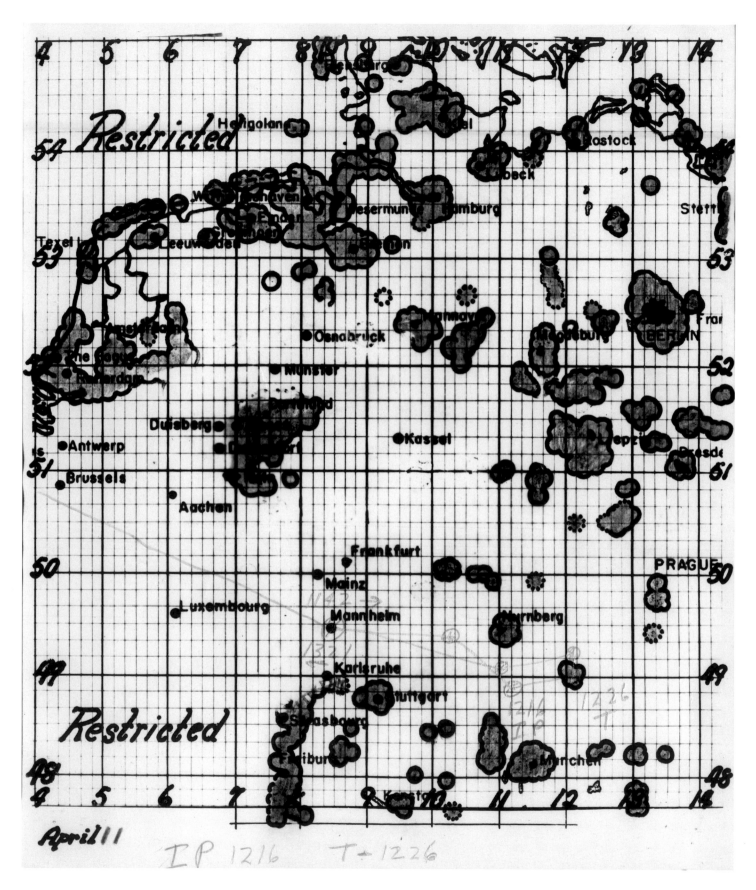

Flak map showing concentrations of flak guns in Germany, to be avoided as much as possible. We had a new map for each mission—we would write our route on each—going to the target and returning home.

B-17 that returned to Great Ashfield with flak damage.
Clarence and Art inspecting the damage.

CHAFF

The Allies were always trying to devise something that would disrupt the German Flak guns and throw them off their targets (our heavy bombers). One thing that someone came up with was chaff. These were bundles of narrow strips of aluminum foil on paper backing tossed from our airplanes over the target. The strips would fall wiggling to the ground to throw off the Flak guns' aiming devices. Since the radio was of little or no use while over the immediate target, the radioman was the designated chaff thrower on each aircraft. The chaff that we dropped benefited the group immediately behind us, and their chaff benefitted the next group behind them; this continued one after another. In the bomber stream, groups followed each other at 3-minute intervals.

On April 19, 1945, we all bombed Hamburg visually since the weather was clear and cloudless. We had no problem seeing the targets. The 385th Group led the 8th Air Force on that mission. Since there were no planes ahead of us over the target to protect us from the Flak guns, we had to do it ourselves. Our crew was one of six airplanes designated as "chaff ships." Instead of regular bombs, each of us carried sixty 100-lb practice bombs filled with chaff with timers set to explode the "bomb" very soon after leaving the airplane. At 30,000 feet we were the first airplanes over the target flying fast and some 2000 feet higher than the group, not in formation, but spread out in a rough line. The "chaff" bombs were dropped at one-second intervals so that we could saturate the area under us long enough for our main group to arrive. This tactic was continued until the end of the war in Europe and seemed to us that it worked very well.

OUR GROUP DIDN'T LOSE ANYBODY ON THIS MISSION!

SLOW TIMING ENGINES

In between flying combat missions, when our crew was on stand down, we were scheduled to fly "slow time" missions. Slow time was always needed to repair or replace engines on our B-17s. Two hours were needed for one engine and four hours were needed for two or more replacements, for breaking them in slowly. We flew with a skeleton crew because there was no danger from enemy fighters so gunners were not needed. There was the pilot, co-pilot, navigator, engineer and radio operator.

We would often fly over Scotland and we would go from one end to the other in our four-hour trips. In two hours we went part way and got to know Scotland very well. I identified Loch Ness (no monsters visible), Loch Lomond ("You take the high road") and other sites of interest.

When we were flying four hours, we often had "observers" with us. Everyone at the base on flying status had to fly at least four hours each month in order to get flight pay, which was 50% added onto the base pay. We would have one "Ground Pounder" on board with us. He kept busy the whole trip writing names and serial numbers of his friends in the flight log. There were 6 people on board but 20 or more names in the flight log! We didn't care at all. We would much rather have one observer instead of a plane load with us.

THE NOSE

While we were flying missions over Western Europe at altitude, we had oxygen checks every few minutes to be sure all of the crew was OK. Since we could not all see each other we had to check in. The pilot would ask for an oxygen check and one by one we would sound off: Roger Tail, Roger Waist, Roger Radio etc. Since Bill Schloss, the bombardier and I were both in the nose, many times when I would be busy navigating he would report for both of us with, Roger Nose.

This got to be a joke with the crew and from then on, Bill was known as The Nose.

"Lucky Bastard Club" is a certificate awarded for completing 25 missions.

THE BOTTLE OF "OLD GRANDAD"

When we were at Savannah, Georgia on our way overseas, our pilot, Clarence Fauber, bought a quart bottle of Old Granddad whiskey. He packed it with his socks and clothing, put it in his B-4 bag and took it overseas to England with us. He saved it to drink when he finished his tour of duty of flying missions or when the war ended, whichever came first. I didn't drink at all then, but told Clarence that if we finished our tours at the same time or were still alive when the war ended, I would have a drink with him.

Fortunately, we just had a few missions to complete our tours when Germany was defeated. We had flown a food drop mission on May 7, 1945, and while we were in the air, word came that Germany had capitulated, and the next day, May 8th was declared V-E Day (Victory in Europe). We had been shot at by the Germans on the ground in Holland, and sustained major battle damage. This was the last combat damage sustained in the 8th Air Force in World War II.

We celebrated the evening of May 7 by breaking out Clarence's bottle of Old Grand Dad. I had my first real drink with him. I've had many drinks since then, but none were as memorable as this one!

MERCY MISSION
LINZ, AUSTRIA TO PARIS, FRANCE

The war in Europe officially ended on May 8, 1945, V-E. Day (Victory in Europe). After celebrating for a short time, and congratulating each other for "STILL ALIVE IN 45", we set about closing our airbase at Great Ashfield, Suffolk, England and returning it to the British. Also, we were preparing our airplanes and equipment for transport back to the old U.S. of A. We were the 385th Bomb Group (heavy) of the 3rd Wing of the 8th Air Force.

Word came that General George Patton (Old Blood and Guts) had liberated a number of French soldiers and civilians in Austria that had been prisoners of the Germans. Many had been held since the war started in 1939 and had been in the work camps. The bridges, roads and railroads all over Germany had been destroyed by the 8th Air Force and ground forces. With little other transportation available, Patton's staff contacted General Jimmy Doolittle's 8th Air Force in England and asked us to transport these former prisoners to France in our B-17 heavy bombers.

On May 25, 1945, a number of B-17s left our base in East Anglia and flew to an improvised airbase just outside Linz, Austria near the Danube River. We flew with a bare-bones skeleton crew so that there would be enough space for the liberated prisoners. Our skeleton crew consisted of:

Pilot and Aircraft Commander: 1st Lt. Clarence E. Fauber of East Chicago, Indiana
Co-Pilot: 2nd Lt. Dale G. Smeltzer, Boseman, Montana
Navigator: 1st Lt. Arthur L. Schaefer, Tucson, Arizona
Engineer: Sgt. Gerald Donnelly, St. Louis, Missouri
Radio Operator: Sgt. James Elder, New England

We left four members of our crew at home at Great Ashfield. They were not needed for this operation because we weren't carrying any bombs and we didn't have to fend off any bandits (enemy fighters).These were:

Lt. William Schloss, Bombardier, Cleveland, Ohio
Sgt. Walter Hatch, Waist Gunner, Duluth, Minnesota
Sgt. John DeMucci, Ball Turret, Philadelphia, Pennsylvania
Sgt. Robert Hake, Tail Turret, Eaton, Ohio

Our airplane, "IN LIKE FLYNN", was the third plane to take off, but the first to land at the Linz airport. Groups of 30 ex-prisoners were lined up at intervals on both sides of the taxi strip. There must have been 30 or more groups. I opened my astrodome on the top of the plane, stood on my navigator's table, and had my head and arms out. I waved to each group as we taxied the length of the strip. Each group waited for my wave and then went wild, jumping up and down and waving their arms. I felt like Lindbergh when he landed in Paris in 1927. This was the biggest thrill of my young life!

After trading souvenirs with the POWs and GIs, we loaded 30 of the liberated prisoners, along with their belongings, into our plane. The other planes in our group followed suit. We had benches installed in the waist compartment and the bomb bays for them. Seven were in the nose with me. We brought candy bars and gum for them--they loved us!! The men were very thin but in good condition from all the hard work they had been forced to do by the Germans.

Clarence Fauber (Pilot) and Dale Smeltzer (Co-Pilot) refused to wear their parachute harnesses, since there were none for our guests. But I wore mine. I was the only one in the nose with a way out in case of trouble. I thought about having to fight them for my chute, but we made the trip without having to test the outcome.

We flew very low on our trip back because our guests had no oxygen. Our crew and guests could see the damage we had done to the cities, bridges, railroads, etc. The cities were just shells of buildings, the bridges were down and most of the railroads were unusable. When we flew over Augsburg, we noticed that the only structures left standing were the flak towers with their 88mm guns. We could see them plainly and we were sure glad that they weren't shooting at us anymore.

I rotated the seven ex-prisoners into the Bombardier's chair in the Plexiglas nose of the airplane so that each could get a good view of Austria, Germany, and France. A number of them had never flown before. They didn't know English, and we didn't know much French but used "sil vou plait" and "Merci beau coup" a lot! Jim Elder (radio operator) kept shuffling the men to and from the bomb bay and the waist, so that all could see the sights. He had to keep them going back and forth to keep the airplane trimmed. If they had all run to the back of the plane at once to look out, Fauber would have had a time keeping the plane on an even keel.

When we crossed the Rhine River near Strasberg, I announced over the intercom that we were now flying over France and when it was communicated to them, all our guests cheered loudly and emotionally with tears in their eyes. Home, to them, had never looked so good!

When we arrived at Paris, Fauber toured the area so that the Frenchmen could see the Seine River, Eiffel Tower, Notre Dame Cathedral and other points of interest. Fauber couldn't resist the temptation to do three pylon turns around the Eiffel Tower (it stands only 1000 feet high). Our plane was in a 90 degree turn for those three revolutions, but nobody in the plane cared and I'm sure the people on the ground thought "There goes those crazy Yanks!" Their much beloved capitol! They were ecstatic! We toured Paris, Versailles, and surrounding vicinity from a bird's eye view for some 25 minutes so that all our guests could get a good look. We landed at Chantilly, about 30 miles north of

Paris. It was raining very hard and Clarence Fauber couldn't see the ground at all. I sat in the Bombardier's chair and directed the plane on the downwind leg and into the landing until the last 300 yards or so. Fauber could then see the ground and we landed OK.

The Frenchmen hugged us, each other, and kissed the ground. We felt like the great emancipators when we returned to our base in England, elated with "Mission Accomplished."

- MERCY -
- MISSION - May 25, 1945

To: LINZ -- Austria

Flew in single ships with skeleton crew -- our skeletons were Fauber, Smeltzer, Donnelly, Elder and Schaefer to Linz to bring back French soldiers that had been prisoners of war of the Germans. Many had been held since the war started in 1939 and had been in the work camps.

Were the 3rd. plane off the ground but were the first to land at an airbase outside Linz. Groups of 30 prisoners each were lined up on both sides of the taxi strip-- I opened the astrodome, stood on my navigator's table and had my head and arms out. I waved to each group as we taxied the length of the strip. Each group waited for my wave and then went wild -- waving and jumping up and down. I felt like Lindbergh when he landed in Paris. This was the biggest thrill of my young life!!

After trading souvenirs with the prisoners, we loaded 30 of them in our plane -- we had benches installed in the bomb bay -- 7 were in the nose with me. We brought sacks of candy bars and gum for them -- they loved us.

Fauber and Smeltzer refused to wear their parachute harnesses but I did -- I was the only one in the nose with a way out in case of trouble. I thought about having to fight them for my chute but we made the trip without incident.

over

(31)

Toured Paris so the prisoners could see the Eiffel Tower, Notre Dame Cathedral, etc. and landed at Chantilly, about 30 miles north of Paris. It was raining and Fauber couldn't see the ground at all. I directed the plane on the downwind leg and into the landing until the last 300 yards or so. Landed O.K. Frenchmen kissed the ground. We unloaded them and went back to England.

11 hours 20 minutes away from Great Ashfield.

115

MERCY MISSION ADDENDUM

In the summer of 2005, the French celebrated the 60th Anniversary of the end of World War II. The transporting of the many POWs from Austria to France, by the 8th Air Force, was a part of this celebration. These prisoners were brought to several airfields in or near Paris.

Chantilly was one of these. The French had rebuilt a B-17 that had crash-landed in France. Its name was "Pink Lady". It probably had crash-landed in France during the war and the United States wrote it off as too costly to get repaired where it was. The French were able to put it all back together and use it for occasions such as this. I don't know if "Pink Lady" was the original name that the Americans gave it or if this was a French creation. "Pink Lady" participated along with the celebrations on the ground with French fly-overs at Chantilly and other airfields.

A number of my friends and veterans of the 385th Bomb Group was on a tour of England and France and participated at Chantilly since many had flown the planes that had brought the prisoners there. I had given a copy of my "Mercy Mission" to the president of our memorial association. The president was Art Driscoll, my second pilot, the one I flew home with. He showed my story to the French officials. They were enthralled with the story and had it translated into French in its entirety for distribution throughout France.

Now I am published in two languages on two continents!!!

COMING IN ON A WING AND A PRAYER

"We're Coming In On A Wing And A Prayer" is a British song from World War II. The Americans adopted it and sang it a lot. It had so much meaning for us flyers of the 8th Air Force.

This was our crew's song. We sang it in the officer's or NCO's clubs and in the barracks, and in the air. Several times we sang it as we returned to Great Ashfield after a tough mission. It always lifted our spirits and fit the moment, which was one of great thankfulness to be alive. I will forever remember singing it!

I will never forget our loyal B-17s that always managed to return us to safety. They provided the ever-trusting wings that brought us home and we provided the belief in prayer that saw us through, time after time.

BY   RICHARD SCHAEFER (GRANDSON)
An Angel on "Navigator Wings"

ON A WING AND A PRAYER (SONG)

We're coming in on a wing and a prayer,

Coming in on a wing and a prayer.

Though there's one engine gone

We will still carry on.

We're coming in on a wing and a prayer.

What a show, what a fight,

Yes, we really hit our target for tonight!

We sing as we limp through the air,

Look below, there's our field over there!

With our full crew aboard

And our trust in the Lord,

We're coming in on a wing and a prayer!

ANDY ROONEY

During World War II in Europe, Andy Rooney and Walter Cronkite were reporters for the Armed Forces newspaper, "THE STARS AND STRIPES".

It so happened that the 385th Bomb Group at Great Ashfield, Suffolk, England (our base) had a B-17 named THE STARS AND STRIPES. The newspaper and the Bomb Group hatched a plan to have Andy fly in it for an actual mission over Germany. He arrived at our base and was immediately given the royal treatment. Since a civilian would be considered a spy and shot if captured, he was given a Battle Field commission before flying. The new lieutenant actually flew two missions with our group to targets well into Germany. He flew as an observer in the nose with the navigator and bombardier, with no bad results. The planes returned from the missions bringing the happy crew and Andy home safely.

Andy became my hero because he flew on these dangerous missions that he didn't have to, as we did. People have criticized him many times for his programs, but I stand by him and his ideas to the end!

LAUNDRY DAY AT GREAT ASHFIELD

About once a month, we would clean all our woolen clothing such as our pants, shirts, blouses (jackets), ties, etc. We took them to the flight line and got a big bucket of 100 Octane gasoline to do the job. There was no color in this gasoline, it was as clear as water. We doused our clothing for sometime and hung it in the sun to dry. No cleaning bills!

Our suntans (shirts and pants), socks, cottons, etc., were done by the local English ladies that had nice little cottage industries in their homes. We took them our clothing every week and picked it up 2 or 3 days later.

With our cleaning and their washing and ironing, we always looked clean and neat!

SUPERSTITIOUS OR NOT!

I never have been superstitious but when we were flying missions, we all seemed to have some things that we thought would be our lucky charms. You may think you are not superstitious, but you don't want to tempt fate or take chances.

I had a silver and onyx ring that my big sister, Kay, had given me. I was wearing it on my first mission and since I had come through it alive, I didn't want to take a chance, so I wore it on all my missions. It worked!!

Also, I had purchased 6 pairs of heavy socks all the same kind and color. I rotated them to wear on all my missions, had them laundered, and recycled them. I never wore any other socks when I flew.

Our Bombardier, Bill Schloss, had a 50-mission hat that he wore or had with him on all his missions. It was dirty because he didn't want to wash the luck out of it. It was wrinkled and folded back so the brass eagle was looking skyward, but it sure kept him safe. On one of the missions, when Bill was not flying, he loaned me his lucky hat for my protection. I wore it, just in case!

Each of us had something similar that warded off bad luck and brought us back to Great Ashfield in one piece.

FOOD AT GREAT ASHFIELD

Great Ashfield
Suffolk, England

The food at the 385. Bomb Group was adequate, not too much variety and with many substitutions from what we were used to in the States. We ate a lot of pork and ham, since the local farmers all raised pigs by the gazillion; powdered eggs and powdered milk. WE also had Spam, lots of potatoes and turnips and rutabagas as big as your head. Besides the pork, about the only fresh meat we had was horsemeat from the big Belgian draft horses that the farmers raised for meat. As I recall, the horse meat was red when cooked, like corned beef and slightly sweet. But we became used to it and began to enjoy it after awhile. We called it "Red Death". I don't recall how it came by the name because it was pretty good.

We always had plenty of coffee in the mess halls or the Officer's snack bar. The Red Cross always had coffee and donuts for us after each mission which was greatly appreciated. That coffee always "hit the spot" after flying in freezing weather at altitude all day!   Anytime we were on leave or off the base, coffee was hard to come by. Tea was plentiful and served so often that we got to enjoy it. We especially liked strong tea when it was mixed half and half with hot milk. All the Britishers had the two pots going at all times, one with tea and the other with hot milk. We enjoyed their crumpets and scones as well.

Fresh eggs were always at a premium and we really savored them when we could get them. On the days that we flew missions, we always had fresh eggs, sausage or spam. I concluded from that, it was generally felt this could be our last meal so they made it as special as they could. Just another daily reminder that our lives were fragile!! A lot of servicemen did not like spam, probably just something to complain about, but I thought it was pretty good if it was fried and still warm. On days that we didn't fly missions, breakfast was powdered eggs scrambled or on toast with sausage or spam. Every week we had homemade cinnamon rolls that were delicious with coffee. We were also treated with jerky or corned beef creamed on toast. This we called "Jerky on a Shingle".

When we were on leave, many of us became friendly with British families. We would visit them and oftentimes have dinner in their homes. Our quarter master, knowing that food was scarce and rationed, would let us take a big bag of food with us to our British friends when we went on leave. This was greatly appreciated and made us more welcome. They treated us like "Ambassadors of Good Will".

DAD'S ENGLISH WALNUTS

When I was in England flying missions in the 8th Air Force, it seemed that we were always hungry. We had our mess that filled us up for awhile, but this never seemed to last. We ate a lot of powdered eggs, spam and horsemeat but we missed a lot of the foods we had enjoyed at home. Our parents would send us boxes of cookies and other goodies that we passed around in our barracks.

My parents were living in California where my Dad worked for a big construction company, helping their blasting crew with the handling of their dynamite, prima cord and other explosives.

One time a box came for me with ten pounds of English Walnuts from California. Apparently there were lots of them where Dad worked so he sent them. Boy were they a welcome sight! We ate all of them and really enjoyed them.

I always thought that was great, getting English Walnuts from California while stationed in England!

"I only regret that I have but one life to give for my country. I'd like to have one left to get home on."

Willie and Joe
Stars and Stripes Armed Forces newspaper, 1945.

ALL HAIL ARIZONA

I always loved to sing. I know a thousand songs by heart and could sing on tune. I never learned to play a musical instrument, except that while I was at the U. of A. before the war, I learned to pick out "All Hail Arizona" on the piano. I learned it by rote and played it with one finger.

This came in handy later, during the war. After becoming an officer, I was transferred from base to base. Each time, upon entering a new base officer's club, I would go over to the piano, which was always there, and pick out "All Hail Arizona." It was surprising how many people I met from Arizona so many miles away, simply through the recognition of a familiar, friendly tune that reminded them nostalgically of home. These moments always developed into mini-reunions.

At Tampa, Tim Ballantyne and I met a captain in the base permanent party who invited us to his home on the beach, on the Gulf of Mexico side of Florida. His wife had also graduated from Arizona so we had a nice reunion.

At Hunter Field, Savannah, Georgia, I ran into a B-17 pilot on his way overseas. He left the day after we met. I never heard of or saw him again. At Goose Bay, Labrador, Canada, I met Joe Sachen, who I had known slightly. He was the base Athletic Officer. We became fast friends. I saw him again when we returned from England after the war in Europe was over, and later at several homecomings at the U. of A.

In England, I continued to play my alma mater's song and met more people from Arizona. In London, at the Grovsener Palace Hotel, which was a gathering place for American servicemen, I met a navigator friend I had known since junior high school, Tucson High School, and the U. of A. We had dinner together and then had to return to our separate bases. The next time I saw him was at one of our high school reunions in Tucson many years later.

After the hostilities were over, and we were back in the states, I was stationed for a short time at Fort Sumner, New Mexico. I played my song and met a captain from Arizona who had received a commission in the cavalry after finishing school and ROTC. He had transferred to the Air Corps and became a pilot. He and I checked out a couple of shotguns from the skeet range and went hunting for cottontail rabbits. Both of us had hunted all our lives and we really enjoyed this. We got several rabbits, cleaned them and asked the base mess officers if they would cook them for us in their kitchen. The cooks fried them in deep fat and they were delicious!! It reminded us of home!

Over the years, I have played ALL Hail Arizona in many hotels, meeting rooms etc., and connected with a number of Arizona Alums.

ALL HAIL ARIZONA!

RADIO CODE NAMES

These names were used to talk to each other while flying a mission in different B-17s and to keep the Germans, who were listening in, from identifying us or our Group. Our Group's code name was Hotshot George and then changed to Clambake George. The Great Ashfield Airbase was called "Hardlife".

COMMAND PERFORMANCE

Peanuts --- Schaefer and crew

Flattop --- Dunlap and crew

Hotnuts --- Schloss

Casanova --- Squeaky Cudizer

Long John ---Jacobson and crew

Whorehouse -- Pitts and crew

Measles -- Red Burr

Louie --- Lundstrom

Dirty Gertie --- Cooper and crew

Jock Strap --- Holmes and crew

Black Jack --- Reed and Crew

Popcorn -- Tarelton Pittard

Blackwood -- Tom Turcott

B – B Eyes -- Driscoll and Crew

88 Keys -- Mike Cepuch

AIRPLANES OF THE 385TH

The crew of the B-17, "Memphis Belle" was the first of the 8th Air Force in England to complete a "tour" of twenty five missions over occupied Europe. There was much ballyhoo and the crew made many appearances all over the United States. At least two movies entitled "Memphis Belle" were made and shown everywhere. The plane was retired from action and toured all over the United States for public viewing. I acquired a photo of it at one of their stops.

The first crew of the 385th to fly twenty five missions was the crew of the "Raunchy Wolf" airplane. "Rum Dum" was the name of the airplane that flew the most missions.

One of our best known planes was "Ruby's Raiders" named for Ruby Newell, the prettiest WAC in the ETO. She was the girlfriend of a pilot who bunked in our Nisson Hut. When he finished his tour and went back to the United States, he left a picture of her on the barrack's bulletin board. This was the one that was reproduced and placed on the nose of his airplane. I rescued this picture and brought it home with me.

The airplane, "Half and Half" was made by our creative and capable mechanical group by combining two wrecked planes. The front half of one was still in good shape and the back half of another was undamaged. The two halves flew a number of additional missions.

As a new replacement crew, we did not have a designated airplane for some time. We flew any plane that was not assigned. We flew a number of different planes on our missions. As we accrued seniority and other crews finished their tours and went home, we inherited an airplane that had been flown by the Pitt's crew named, "Is this S-trip really necessary?". On the nose was a scantily clad girl removing her clothing. We called the plane "Queenie" and flew a number of missions in it.

Later we were given a brand new airplane for our own. We named it "In Like Flynn".

OTHER PLANES IN OUR GROUP WERE:

Hot Chocolate	Maiden America
Hell's Belles	Mission Belle
Big Gas Bird	Hustlin Hussy
Lil' Audry	Homesick Angel
Leading Lady	Vapor Trail Joe
Gypsy	Latest Rumor
Closz Call	Joker
Madam Shoo Shoo	Slo Joe
Satan's Mate	Honey Bee
Target for Tonight	Sioux Princess
Round Trip Ticket	Raggedy Ann
Lenora Linda	
There were many more	

Ruby Newell. She was voted the prettiest WAC in the ETO. Girlfriend of a captain in our barracks.

Art and Bill Schloss with Ruby's Raiders B-17.

Art, Clarence Fauber, and Bill Schloss by one of our veteran airplanes, Hells Belles.

Clarence and Bill by Sioux Princess airplane.

Clarence and Art by Maiden America B-17.

Memphis Bell B-17-F on tour.

B-17G "I'll Be Around" at the Pima Air Museum in Tucson.

June 19, 1945

To: HOME!!!

With Driscoll and crew -- had 20 people total
in our plane, including Lt. Colonel Charles
Reid, our squadron Commander, Jackie Palmer,
squadron navigator (my back up), 2 engineers,
3 crew chiefs, etc.

Flew to Valley, Wales, spent the night
and then on to Iceland.

Landed at Reykjavik on the southwest
corner of Iceland on June 20, 1945. It
stayed light all night -- we saw the sun
near the horizon all the time -- it never set.

Left Iceland and went to Goose Bay,
Laborador on June 21, 1945. Saw my friend
from Arizona, Joe Sachen, who was still stationed
at Goose Bay -- he was the base athletic
officer. The weather was nice, but the
gnats tried to make off with our radio operator.

Flew to Bradley Field, Massachusetts,
just out of Boston, on June 22, 1945, just
5 months, 2 weeks since leaving the old
U.S.of A.

HOME!! -- STILL ALIVE IN 45!!

(33)

COMING HOME

After V-E Day, on May 8, 1945, the war was over and our group was preparing to return to the states. Plans were to regroup and maybe train in B-29s and go to the Pacific to fight the Japanese . These plans never materialized, McArthur didn't need any more B-29 groups for the war in the Pacific. We set about getting our planes in tip-top shape for the flight home and getting all of our equipment ready to ship.

General Jimmie Doolittle's 8th Air Force High Command felt that we shouldn't just sit on our hands, but should keep up with our training. To keep from getting rusty, Navigators were given tests to keep their skills up to snuff. On the first test, I made 100% and tied for first place in all the 8th Air Force with a navigator in our group. On the second test, I made 98% and tied for third.

Because we had no schedule for our departure from Great Ashfield, our pilot, Clarence Fauber, and many other crew members elected to go home by ship instead of waiting for our mass exodus with our planes and equipment. Clarence was the only married member of our crew and he wanted to get home as soon as possible. As it turned out, he had to wait for a ship, and those of us that flew home with the group got home sooner than he did.

For the trip home, each B-17 was to carry as much equipment as it could as well as many crew members and "Ground Pounders" (non-flying staff or maintenance people) as we had room for. Our Squadron Commander, Colonel Charles Reid handpicked a crew to fly him home. Art Driscoll was chosen as the pilot and I was chosen navigator. I believe he chose me based on the high scores I made on the Navigator's tests and the 27 missions I had flown without getting lost once. He picked the Squadron Navigator, Jackie Palmer, as my back-up. We had 2 co-pilots, 2 bombardiers, 2 radio operators, 2 engineers, 3 crew chiefs, etc.

We left Great Ashfield on June 19, 1945 and flew to Valley, Wales, spent the night and then flew up the West coast of Scotland and on to Reykjavik, Iceland, where we spent the night. June 20th is the summer solstice and is the longest day of the year. It stayed daylight all night, the sun stayed near the horizon and never set. We went into Reykjavik and saw that the people were much happier than they were the last time we were there. The war was over and their homeland, Denmark, was free of the Germans.

Art Driscoll, Jack Sweeney (bombardier) and I went all over Reykjavik observing how the locals lived and worked. The little Icelandic horses were out on the hillsides eating mosses and grasses instead of the fish heads that they lived on all winter. Almost all of the people were blondes and there were only a few red heads. Our co-pilot, Joe Backus, got into trouble by showing too much interest in an Icelandic lady and four of her brothers took exception to this. They were huge, burly fishermen and we wanted no part of them. We were able to spirit Joe away before he got us into a brawl, which I am sure we would have lost.

We left Iceland the next morning and went to Goose Bay, Labrador, Canada. Again we flew over the southern part of Greenland. My friend, Captain Joe Sachen from Arizona, was still the base athletic officer at Goose Bay. Joe's younger brother was a POW of the Germans and I was able to allay his fears and worries by reporting that the POWs were in very good shape, thinner perhaps, but healthy. I had breakfast with Joe and almost missed our briefing for the last leg of our journey home. Fortunately, Captain Palmer covered the briefing for me and we had no difficulty navigating our plane to Bradley Field, Connecticut, just outside of Boston. WE WERE HOME AND STILL ALIVE IN '45!!!! Just 5 months and 17 days since we left the old U. S of A to go overseas. We were taken to Boston for processing, then scattered to our respective processing centers for our scheduled triple R, (Rest, Rehabilitation and Recuperation). I went to Fort Bliss, Texas, and then went home to Tucson. I got home about July 8th.

"COMING HOME"

Peace and rest at length have come

All the day's long tale is past

And each heart is whispering

Home, Home at last!!

By Thomas Hood

From Stars and Stripes Armed Forces newspaper.

FORT SUMNER

The war in Europe officially ended on May 8, 1945 (V-E Day).

After celebrating and bringing the French prisoners from Austria to Chantilly, France, I flew home with the 385th Bomb Group to Bradley Field, Connecticut. Then we went by train to Fort Bliss, Texas and were given a 30-day R and R (rest and recuperation) leave that I spent in Tucson. A number of my friends were also home. We spent many afternoons at the Arizona Inn swimming pool and our evenings at the Double R or the Santa Rita Hotel. We had a great time!

I then went back to Fort Bliss and then I was sent to Sioux Falls, South Dakota for reassignment. I was on the train on August 14, 1945, somewhere between Fort Bliss and Sioux Falls, when word came that Japan had surrendered and August 14th was then declared V-J Day! We all hooped and hollered but couldn't get off the train to celebrate properly. I reasoned that I had celebrated V-E Day in England and that would have to be enough.

I spent several days at Sioux Falls, and then I was sent to Fort Sumner, New Mexico for further reassignment. Fort Sumner was an army base in Baca County located in the wide open spaces between Roswell and Tucumcari. Its only claim to fame was that Billy the Kid (William Bonney) was killed there by sheriff Pat Garret near the end of the notorious Lincoln County War in the 1800s. His grave was the centerpiece of the town. I have no idea why we fly-boys were sent there. There was a large compound for German prisoners of war as part of the base. This was a minimum security facility with a 12 foot no-climb fence around several two-story army barracks. These prisoners were well screened and considered non-violent and not escape risks. They were treated so good that a lot of them didn't want to go back to Germany. Many were assigned to jobs around the base. Some were gardeners, while others worked in the kitchens or at other menial jobs.

As usual, when I went to the officer's club I played "All Hail Arizona." A captain immediately came over, told me he was an Arizona grad that had been commissioned in the horse cavalry through R.O.T.C. He then transferred to the Army Air Corps , and became a pilot in the 8th Air Force. He had been born and raised in Arizona as I was, so we hit it off very well.

One evening, we decided to check out some skeet guns and a couple of boxes of birdshot and go hunting for cottontail rabbits. We would hunt only on the base, so licenses weren't needed and there were no wardens to worry about. We got three rabbits, cleaned them and asked the mess officer if he would have the kitchen cook them for us; which they did and they were deliciously deep-fried!! We really enjoyed them and realized that they were almost a forgotten taste!! The other officers in our BOQ (Bachelor Officers' Quarters) asked us if we would go out again and shoot some more so that they could enjoy them also. We went out the next morning. As we walked past the POW stockade, there was a number of POWs in the yard watching us. Suddenly, a rabbit jumped out of the bushes just ahead of us and ran away from the fence. Both of us unlimbered our shotguns and shot at him. We fired at the same time; the rabbit went head over heels, dead. We never knew which one of us (or both) got him. We looked around and the POWs were wide-eyed and gawking! My friend muttered something like "that will show them," and we continued on our way. We hunted along a dry wash that had all sorts of desert growth and got five rabbits and four quail between us. We brought them back, cleaned them and had them cooked for us. Our BOQ had a banquet that night.

We were at Fort Sumner for a few weeks, and then we were assigned to various Air Bases all over the country. I requested and got assigned to Davis-Monthan in Tucson for B-29 training. I spent the last few months of my military career there as a test crew navigator on B-29s. Then I left active duty and went back to the University of Arizona to get my degree in mining engineering.

From Stars and Stripes Armed Forces newspaper of 1945.

THERE'S ALWAYS

A TOMORROW

Art at home in Tucson, sharing quiet time with friends.

TOMORROW

My life took a major turn toward wonderful and fulfilling chapters of great experiences, people, family and accomplishments; some filled with educating failures and many others that became rewarding lessons.

Among the many important things in my life I must share with you, are the lives of my devoted crew; some still here and most gone and tell you what a few were to become and do. They must be mentioned for they were a gallant bunch of patriots and comrades.

EVERY ENDING IS A NEW POINT OF BEGINNING

Louise L. Hay

Mary Esther and Art at a Ranch cookout —Tucson.

RETURN TO CIVILIAN LIFE

All the members of our crew returned to civilian life and settled right in. We were all happy and proud that we had done our bit for our country and helped win the war.

Clarence Fauber became a professor of Mechanical Engineering at Indiana State University in Terre Haute.

Dale Smeltzer became a professor of Agriculture at the University of California at Davis.

Bill Schloss was a businessman in Cleveland, Ohio and then retired to Florida.

Gerry Donnelly went to Miami, Florida where he lived for many years. He was the 385th Bomb Group Historian for a number of years.

Jim Elder left Haverhill, Massachusetts and moved to St. Petersburg, Florida.

Johnny Demucci married his long time sweetheart Marty and they lived in Philadelphia for many years. Later they moved to Egg Harbor, New Jersey where they now live.

Walter Hatch returned to Duluth, Minnesota. He died at an early age and was the first of our crew to go.

Bob Hake became a journeyman machinist and then became a contractor with his sons, building houses in Eaton, Ohio.

I got my degree in Mining Engineering at the University of Arizona. My first job after graduation was with Union Carbide in the Uranium mines and mills in Colorado. Then I traveled all over the Western Hemisphere from Newfoundland to Peru, inspecting mines, mills and smelters for ASARCO, (American Smelting and Refining Company). My wife, Mary Esther, accompanied me for many years on most of these trips. After retiring, I was invited to become an adjunct mining professor at the University of Arizona. Then, I retired again and worked for my wife as a framer and Art critic!!

THE GHOSTS OF WAR RETURN

After sixty eight years the chills of fear still run through my body. Just recently, the other day, as I stood waiting at a counter of a shop here in Tucson, a nice man who works there, approached and offered his services. When he stood front and center to me, I noticed the shirt he was wearing had the name "Swinefurt"in very large letters. This was a German city that the 8th Air Force had bombed. "Swinefurt" was the ball-bearing center for all of Germany and the 8th Air Force really wanted to knock it out. The Luftwaffe came up with all their might and our air force lost more than sixty B-17s on that one mission, over six hundred of our men were lost in a single day. Chills and goose bumps appeared on my arms while I recalled the whole memory. The man stood waiting patiently for me to ask for his services. I had to stand quietly for a moment to regain my composure.

I suppose that this is what is referred to as post-traumatic stress. The memories of war stay with you forever!

No Milk Run Here

U.S. Army Air Force Photo

From the Stars and Stripes Armed Forces newspaper April 12, 1945.

OHIO AIR FORCE GOLDEN GOOSE THUNDERBIRD WANDERING DUCHESS CURLY'S KIDS
SKY GODDESS ROUNDTRIP TICKET PICCADILLY QUEEN BLUE CHAMPAGNE MARY ELLEN DRAGON LADY
SALLY B RAUNCHY WOLF CHOWHOUND YANK GELDING WINNIE THE POOH
HONKY TONK SAL "HAYBAG" ANNIE MISS AMERICA STARS AND STRIPES
HESITATIN' HUSSY PREGNANT PORTIA DORSAL QUEEN WAR WEARY
BIG GAS BIRD LIBERTY BELLE HUSTLIN' HUSSY LEADING LADY ALEXANDER'S RAGTIME BAND
ANGELS SISTER LI'L AUDREY LONESOME POLECAT HARES BREATH
STAR DUST MARY PAT SLY FOX
MR. SMITH
SKY CHIEF TARGET FOR TONIGHT SHACK N LADY
MR. LUCKY PERRY'S PIRATES SLO JO JUNIOR OL' DOODLE BUG
GIZMO SACK TIME
MADAME SHOO SHOO ROGER THE DODGER RAGGED BUT RIGHT SWEET CHARIOT
PAT PENDING IMPATIENT VIRGIN SWINGING DOOR
POSSIBLE STRAIGHT MICKY RUBY'S RAIDERS MISSISSIPPI MISS
HALF AND HALF SLEEPYTIME GAL
ROUNDTRIP JACK HOMESICK ANGEL LATEST RUMOR MAIDEN AMERICA LULU BELLE
SHACK BUNNY MY GAL SAL MISSION BELLE SLICK CHICK
SPIRIT OF CHICAGO BIG STINKY VIBRANT VIRGIN OL' RUM DUM FOOLISH VIRGIN
SOUTHERN BELLE RAGGEDY ANNE MAC'S HACK
VAT 69 YANK CRASH WAGON III RAGGED BUT RIGHT
MARY ELLEN III HOT CHOCLATE LIL-LU STORK CLUB LADY ANN AIN'T MISBEHAVIN' MARY ELLEN II
IN LIKE FLYNN

HARD LIFE HERALD

NEWSLETTER OF THE
385th BOMBARDMENT GROUP MEMORIAL ASSOCIATION

G

COMBAT UNITS
HQ. SQUADRON
548th BOMB SQ.
549th BOMB SQ.
550th BOMB SQ.
551st BOMB SQ.

VOL. XVIII, NO. 5
Editor: Ed Stern
Printed by Interstate Printing
Fargo, North Dakota

SEPTEMBER 1991

SUPPORT UNITS
424th AIR SVS. GP.
877th CHEM. CO. (AO)
DET. 155, 18th AWS
31st STATION COMPLEMENT SQ.

IN LIKE FLYNN

B-17-G Flying Fortress

Flown and named by 1st Lt. Clarence Fauber's crew - 549th. Squadron, 385th. Bomb Group (Heavy). Based at Great Ashfield, Suffolk, England. Crew flew 25 missions before V-E Day - May 8, 1945 not including four food drop missions to Holland (Operation Chowhound). Flew to Linz, Austria to bring liberated French POWs of the Germans to Paris.

IN LIKE FLYNN flew home with the Group in June, 1945 and was ultimately scrapped at Kingman, Arizona in 1946. This big gas bird did her job well.

Crew:

Clarence Fauber	Pilot
Dale Smeltzer	Co-Pilot
Arthur Schaefer	Navigator
William Schloss	Bombardier
Gerald Donnelly	Engineer
James Elder	Radio Operator
John DeMucci	Ball Turret Gunner
Walter Hatch	Waist Gunner
Robert Hake	Tail Gunner

At the reunion in Tulsa in June, a photoprint of an original oil painting of a 385th B-17 "IN LIKE FLYNN" was raffled off to benefit All Saints Church in Great Ashfield. The original painting, oil on linen, was done by Mary Schaefer, wife of "IN LIKE FLYNN'S" navigator, Art Schaefer. "IN LIKE FLYNN" was flown and named by Clarence Fauber's crew of the 549th. Sqdn. in 1945.

If any members of the group would like a photo print of "IN LIKE FLYNN", they can be obtained from:

Mary L. Schaefer
2602 E. Windsor
Tucson, AZ 85716
Phone: (602) 795-1309

A MEMORIAL TO THE 385TH BOMBARDMENT GROUP OF THE U.S. 8TH AIR FORCE ALL SAINTS CHURCH

The little centuries old stone All Saints Church in the small community of Great Ashfield in Suffolk was very dear to our 385th Bomb Group. Over the years that we were there from 1942 to 1945 many of the flyers, as well as non-flyers attended services there. When the war in Europe ended and we left England, it was decided to make the church our memorial project. Our group has supported the church all these years and still do with a trust fund.

A small memorial chapel, in the east wing, is dedicated to the 385th Bomb Group. It has an altar and reredos (ornamentally carved screens behind an altar) carved in solid oak. A beautiful, silk American flag hangs permanently in this holy sanctuary. There is a large hand-embossed book with the names of the 400 plus flyers killed in action while flying out of Great Ashfield.

Our group donated a substantial gift to have a stained glass window installed in the chapel. It has the symbol of our group with our motto, "Ales Victoria". There is also the "Square G" and red checker board of our tail markings and the three trees that were a visible landmark of our airfield. A depiction of bombers flying out of a Suffolk sky also appears. A number of doves in the sky reminds us of the P-51 fighters that escorted us on our missions to keep us safe from enemy aircraft.

My wife, Mary Esther, is an artist. She painted an oil painting of our crew's plane, "In Like Flynn", as an anniversary gift to me. Mary and I took a framed 24 x 30 print of this painting to the Group Reunion at Tulsa, Oklahoma in 1991. It was raffled off to benefit the All Saints Church in Great Ashfield. As I recall, it brought in $1200 or more toward the support of the church. The print of the painting has since been distributed to many in the 385th Bomb Group. They have enjoyed it with many memories and with deep gratitude and pride.

Mary has always felt a deep connection and a sense of worth to have been a small part of helping the young men who fought, for all generations to come, to be remembered to their church forever (see attached Bomb Group Newsletter).

490 BG

food and freedom

OPERATION CHOWHOUND 1th - 8th MAY 1945

A TRIBUTE TO THE 8th UNITED STATES ARMY AIR FORCE

452 BG

385 BG

After the fierce winter of 1944-1945 the inhabitants of the still German-occupied Western part of the Netherlands were at the brim of starvation. Having supported the Allies by going on strike the Dutch Railways prevented the enemy from sending troops to the battle zone during Operation Market-Garden in September 1944. In retaliation the Germans denied the people of the Netherlands the same means of transportation to carry badly needed food from the agricultural east to the densely populated west of the country. After pleas by Her Majesty Queen Wilhelmina of the Netherlands to President Franklin Delano Roosevelt and Prime-Minister Sir Winston Churchill General Dwight D.Eisenhower, Supreme Commander Allied Expeditionary Forces was ordered to arrange for relief. Bomber Command, Royal Air Force and the 8th American Army Air Force were detailed to carry out missions of mercy to save the Dutch. Between 1st and 8th May Boeing B17 Flying Fortresses flew 2189 missions, dropping 4,155.6 tons of food at nine drop zones.

95 BG

The people of the Netherlands gratefully acknowledge the help provided by the men who fought to free mankind and who finished their war by bringing salvation rather than destruction. Thanks to their efforts millions of people survived in freedom once again.

385 BG

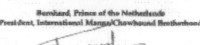

we will never forget.

Bernhard, Prince of the Netherlands
President, International Manna/Chowhound Brotherhood

On behalf of the Food and Freedom Foundation

388 BG

34 BG

190 BG

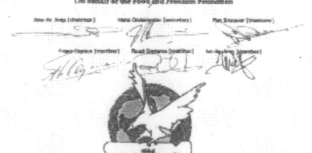
193 SC

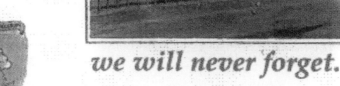

Group insignias of the eleven 8th Air Force groups that participated in the food drop. The 385th was the only group that had the Red Checkerboard tail markings.

LIEUTENANT ART DRISCOLL
PILOT

My thirteenth mission turned out to be a "lucky" one for me!

The weather was so terrible that few of our bomb group found the proper assembly point over Buncher Thirteen. Many of us just joined whatever group in the bomber stream that was headed for Germany. We hit our primary target, an ordnance warehouse north of Berlin. The weather was so bad we broke off with the formation and headed home, alone.

Our navigation instruments were out, so flying through the heavy overcast on instruments over France made us drop down hoping to find a landmark before crossing the English Channel.

The next thing we knew, all HELL broke out as our plane was riddled by flak and ground fire! We realized that we were over Dunkerque, the only German stronghold remaining in that area of France. It had been by passed by the Allies while liberating France.

We had lost much of the control of our Flying Fortress so I made a quick decision not to attempt crossing the Channel but to make a slow, gradual turn back over France. Our tail gunner was badly wounded when flak hit that section of the plane. He could not bail out, so we decided to land in France. We found an RAF base and landed. The plane had some hundred holes in it, some big enough to crawl through. That plane never flew again.

Our tail gunner lost the use of his arms due to his wounds. The RAF returned the crew to our base in England the next day. We used photos from our camera to convince the debriefing officers that we had hit our target even though we didn't bring our plane back.

We were lucky to be alive!!!

TOLD BY HIS WIDOW, MARY DRISCOLL

1st Lt. Art Driscoll, My 2nd Pilot. We flew home together after the war ended.

SERGEANT BOB HAKE
TAIL GUNNER

Bob always spoke of the crew as family; they looked after him, even though they were two and three years older. I have met many of the crew members and their families, and they are wonderful people.

After the war was over, Bob came home to help his family on the farm. He was the oldest boy of nine children. Bob had been home for two and a half years when we met at a dance, I was seventeen. A year later we were engaged and then married two years later in 1951.

A few years later we bought a farmhouse and lived on it for nine years, at which time we had ten children. We sold the farmhouse and Bob and his four sons built our next home. Our eleventh and final child was born in 1967. We sold the home and built a large house for our family of eleven children.

Our daughter was killed in an accident while stationed in the Philippines for the Navy in 1981.

Bob died in July 2006 and is buried at Mount Hill Union Cemetery.

TOLD BY HIS WIDOW, JUANITA HAKE

Bob Hake, our tail gunner and his wife Juanita.

NEVER TO FORGET!!

When our country, the Netherlands, was attacked by the German Forces on May 10, 1940, we were children and grew up in a very hostile surrounding, as the Germans took control over our way of living, forcing many of our country men to work in their plants and factories, on penalty of being imprisoned. Many, many of the Jews, living in our country, were forcefully picked up and deported to Germany, put in concentration camps and killed.

A war is always horrible and World War II was certainly no exception and many lives of people all over the world were sacrificed under sad and terrible circumstances.

In our case, the last period of the German occupation (from September 1944 until May 1945), due to the unsuccessful attempt by the Allied Forces to capture the bridges over our big rivers, life in the Northern part of the Netherlands, which had the big majority of its people, became very, very difficult as to heat, electricity, food etc. They were no longer available in sufficient supply. In many cases, people starved to death or died because of the cold.

But finally towards the end of April and beginning of May, 1945, we got new hope. Suddenly, the Allied Forces flew their little planes over our big cities dropping their food packages with so much needed bread, canned milk, meat, etc. even some chocolate!!! People were standing on the roofs or in the streets to celebrate and wave with tremendous joy to the crews of the planes that flew maybe 150-200 meters over our heads.

For many years, we are now living in Tucson and were enormously pleased to meet with Art Schaefer, one of the crew members on the "food planes" and to be able to express our gratitude to him personally. Art and Mary became good friends and we hope to continue our friendship for many years to come.

Tucson, Nov. 11, 2012   Wilhelmina and Frank Van Veenendaal

Frank and Willy Van Veenendaal at Yosemite.

A reunion of our Bomb Group in Tucson, 1995.
(Left to right) Bob Hake, Clarence Fauber, Harry Woltman,
Norma Woltman, Art Drescoll, Art Schaefer.

*Art and Marvin Borodkin ready to fly in Air Force
Reserve at Davis Monthan — 1946.*

THE BARBER SHOP

In the spring of 1946, the war was over and a lot of us were back in school, at the University of Arizona. One day, my buddy Marvin Borodkin needed a haircut, so we went to the University Barber Shop on the square at 3rd Street and Park Avenue. I didn't need one but waited for Marvin.

At the barber shop, there was an elderly black fellow that shined shoes in a little stand in the corner. He was sick that day, and no one was manning the shoe shine booth. A fellow came in and said he really needed a shoe shine, as he had a big date that night. From my days in the cavalry, one thing I could do well was shine shoes, so I said, "Get up there, I'll shine them for you."

I was popping the cloth and shining away when a friend of ours came by. He was a friend who had been a Sergeant in the infantry in Italy and Germany. He had been wounded several times and he thought little of those softies, the fly boys. He announced in a loud voice, "That's what I like to see, an air corps officer back at his old job!"

The fellow having his shoes shined said, "Is that true?" I told him I was an air corps officer but that this wasn't my regular job. He gave me a dollar! Shines then cost twenty cents. Before his shoes were done, another customer came in for a shine and waited his turn. I shined three pairs of shoes by the time Marvin had gotten his haircut. I had $2.50 which happened to be the price of two pitchers of beer at the Rio Rita Gardens Bar, the Double R, as it was known in those days.

GLOSSARY OF TERMS

MAE WEST: An inflatable, rubberized canvas life preserver worn by all airmen. It was inflated with a small canister of CO_2. It could be kept inflated by mouth.

PFF: the acronym for Path Finder Force, it was a new radar that was crude and not reliable at this time. It was carried by special airplanes, usually one or two in each group.

FLAK: It was German anti-aircraft, of mostly 88mm cannons but some where 105mm and 155mm. The projectiles exploded into shrapnel that could bring down an airplane.

FLAK HELMETS: Huge pot-shaped helmet with bowl-shaped ear flaps held on with leather straps that were worn while over the target, along with the flak vests(front and back protection).

BANDITS: The bandits were enemy aircraft. They were mostly ME-109s and FW-190s in Europe.

TAIL END CHARLIE: the last section of airplanes in low squadron in group formation.

DUNKERQUE/ DUNKIRK: a small pocket of Germans on the French coast that was by-passed by the allies while liberating France. They had flak guns and the area had to be skirted by our planes.

CORRIDOR: These were specific routes for our planes to follow while dropping food to the Dutch. As long as we stayed in these lanes, the Germans were instructed not to shoot at us.

ETA: This was the Estimated Time of Arrival at the target.

IP-INITIAL POINTS: This is where the bomb run to the target was started and the group got into bombing formations.

RP-RALLY POINT: A place where the group returned to flying formation after dropping bombs.

PILOTAGE: This is a navigation method by seeing the ground.

KNOTS: They are nautical miles per hour.

GEE BOX: This was a British method of navigation using radar.

LORAN: It is a "Long Range Aid" to Navigation.

PEASHOOTER JOCKEYS: These were our fighter pilots that escorted the bombers.

COLORS OF THE DAY: These were various colors of flares used for identification to friendly air craft, the P-51s. The colors were changed every day.

OG: He was the Officer of the Guard.

CHAFF: They were strips of aluminum foil on paper used to foul up the German Flak guns' radar.

RUNAWAY PROP: This was an unintentional speeding-up of the engine like an accelerator sticking down.

CONTRAILS: They are vapor trails left by warm engines flying through saturated air, mist.

HELGOLAND: A small island off the coast of Denmark that was occupied by the Germans and had to be avoided. There were many flak guns there that had to be avoided by our planes.

BUNCHER 13: A radio beacon used by the 385th bomb group to assemble our airplanes into formation before each mission. Each group had its own Buncher.

BOMBER STREAM: A parade of bomb groups following each other to the targets. Usually there were three minute intervals between groups.

SALVO: A bomb load dropped all at once.

BOMBS IN TRAIN: A load of bombs dropped at calculated intervals.

MAJOR BATTLE DAMAGE: The damage to a plane that rendered it impossible to be repaired quickly so it could fly the next mission.

STAGING: The assembling and training of crew members from various disciplines to make cohesive working units.

TAIL MARKINGS: An identification method of each group for P-51s to tell which group they were to protect on each mission. The 385th had a yellow tail with a white square and a black "G" prominently place in the middle of it. Later, it became a red checkerboard design.

OPERATION CHOWHOUND: This was the food drop into Holland near the end of the war. MANNA is what the British called the food drop.

MILK RUN: An easy and safe mission with little or no Flak or Enemy fighters.

TRACER: A bullet with a red flare instead of a projectile.

NAPALM: Bombs filled with jellied gasoline used to set fires on enemy installations.

IFF: Radio signals indicating Information, Friend or Foe. They were sent out to the British Coast Guard while returning to England from a mission to identify us as friends, not attacking German airplanes.

SLOW TIMING: This was done while breaking in replaced engines.

FLAK VEST: The body armor designed to protect crew members while they were over target.

STAND DOWN: Time when you were not scheduled to fly.

BLOUSES: These were the army dress uniform jackets.

BROWSE: It consisted of grasses, mosses and all natural food meant for the animals.

V1s and V2s: These were German missiles shot at England from the occupied Dutch coast. The V1s were low-flying buzz bombs and V2s were high altitude missiles shot at random toward London.

SORTIE: This was one airplane, one mission.

BOQ: The name given to the bachelor officer's quarters.

TRIMMING: Keeping the airplane balanced as the loads changed, such as when dropping bombs, using fuel, or crew moving around.

LAND-FALL: A method of navigation where you purposely aim either right or left of your destination point and then turn when a natural guide such as a shoreline, river, etc., appears.

OCTANT: A navigation instrument like a sextant but not as sensitive. It only covered one eighth of a circle whereas the sextant covered one sixth.

ETO: Acronym for European Theater of Operations.

WAC: Women's Army Corps. They were women who were in the military but not in actual combat.

MY FAMILY

Schaefer Family: Nancy, Richard, Mary Esther, Cheri, and Art in our backyard in Tucson.

THE CHILDREN'S LOVE
FOR THEIR FATHER

MY DAD IS THE GREATEST DAD IN THE WORLD!
BY NANCY SCHAEFER CASEY

My dad has always been there for my brother, sister and me. He protected us when we were young and if we needed his help for any reason he has been there for us.

We use to go fishing and have picnics on Sundays by a stream or a lake. He taught us how to fish and hunt. We had a special picnic spot by Ruby Lake, which was a private lake owned by friends of ours.   I will never forget the Sunday we arrived at our favorite picnic spot, and there was an enormous white bull standing there! My dad, who has never been afraid of anything that I experienced, started shooing the bull away with his hat! He yelled at the bull and kept saying shoo! Finally, this huge animal started moving in the direction my dad wanted him to. He was about 100 feet from us when two cowboys showed up and lassoed him! They told my dad that, that bull had killed a few men not too long ago who got too close to him!!!! My dad never exhibited any fear even after being told that. If he had known that before-hand he would have done the same thing. Our picnic spot was important to us. He had a history going back to when I was a baby of doing this very same thing!

When we were little my dad built a swing set for us out of heavy pipe and made the swings out of wood. He made us a teeter totter out of a plank of wood and metal pipe as well. He made anything we needed. He made me a rocking horse for Christmas and my mother painted it. In fact, he made all of their friends a rocking horse for their daughters, who were my age! It was quite a Christmas! I think he made 5 rocking horses in all. He taught us how to ride a bike, and how to go downhill on a sled and a disk. We always had a lot of fun together.

If it wasn't for my dad I would never have passed Algebra in high school. He was a Mining Engineer so math was easy for him. He would spend hours every evening trying to help me understand it. I finally passed the class because he spent endless time helping me. He was head of safety for A.S.A.R.CO Mining Company, so he traveled all over North, Central and South America inspecting the mines, smelters and refineries. He often composed diagrams of safety devices, had them made and installed, where he felt they were needed. His job was to keep everyone safe. He often met and conferred with OSCHA in order to keep A.S.A.R.CO in safety compliance.

One Saturday, he took us out to the A.S.A.R.CO open pit he worked at . He drove his little Volkswagen beetle bug out there that day to dramatize something for us we were later to find out. We got out of the car and he drove it under one of the big dump trucks! We have a great picture of our little car under the big truck. We spent a few hours our there as dad gave us a tour of the plant. He timed our trip to coincide with that day's blasting, so we were able to see that! What an experience that was! As an additional treat, he brought home the inner tube from one of those large trucks tires and inflated it as soon as we got home. We always wanted a trampoline so this was perfect! My sister and I could be found jumping on this inner tube for hours after school in the afternoons. We put it under a tree in our backyard and would jump so hard we would land in the tree. It was so much fun!

He loved to fish whether it was for trout or the larger fish in the sea . I remember when we went deep sea fishing in Guaymas. We pulled up many Yellow Tail Tuna, and Red Snapper, along with an eel, and a porcupine fish! He was always so capable no matter where we were and we always had a ball! We also loved to go to the White Mountains to hike and fish.

We learned to target shoot when we were young. He taught us all of the safety rules. He has won many contests for his target shooting including one recently at the big Elkhorn Ride. Many men arrive from all over the world and they spend a fortune on their guns and equipment. Dad brought his dad's shot gun, which was 100 years old! He looked like Davy Crockett out there. They were laughing at him and guess who won? My dad of course! You can believe they gave him respect after that! He would take my brother hunting for rabbit or quail every year. I didn't like to kill anything so he stopped taking me. We always had what they killed for dinner that night.

When I was little we lived in Colorado, he would go hunting every winter for deer. The deer he killed would feed us during the winter. He would kill three deer and give the meat away from two of them, to poor families. He hung the meat in the cellar, covered with cheese cloth, to dry. He would often stay awake at night down there with his rifle, because the cats in the neighborhood would come in through a window and try and eat our meat!

He has always tried to help everyone in any way that he can. He loves us dearly and we love him the same way. We treasure our time together. We have learned so much from him. He has a saying for everything. I find myself saying these little idioms all the time and finally they make sense to me. He set the bar high for us and has led by his example in being: kind, strong, loving, loyal and always a giving person. We owe him a lot! He is our treasure! He is my Hero!!!!

MY FATHER

My father, Art Schaefer, is one of the greatest blessings in my life. A former navigator and World War II hero, as well as a mining engineer, formed a man who cherished his family above all else. He is a compassionate, gentle man who taught us the most valuable lessons in life: to love one another, give to others and never take one another for granted. He taught us to reach for the stars, work hard and strive to be the best. We always knew he would be there to support, comfort, guide and protect us.

My Dad always makes me smile and laugh as he loves to add levity to life by way of a joke, play on words or singing a song. I will always treasure the many trips in the car that he would break out in a song to keep our minds off the miles we had left to travel. Whether it was the stories he would read to me when I was sick or building projects outside together, he always made me feel special and loved. There is no measurement great enough to measure the worth of my father.

Through my Dad's loyalty, dedication and sacrifice we have the freedom to dream, the aspirations to achieve our goals and to love without reservation. We hope that we have instilled these values in our children. My Dad is my hero and one of the two most important people in the world to me.

Thank you Papa, for believing in me, being proud of me for my accomplishments, loving me unconditionally and for standing by my side when I made mistakes or failed. I love you with all my heart!

Your loving daughter,

Cheri Schaefer Romanoski

MY FATHER IS THE GREATEST GIANT

Sir Isaac Newton once said of himself, "If I have seen further than other men, it is because I have stood upon the shoulders of giants." My father is the greatest giant whose shoulders I stand upon and I owe all my successes to him and my Mom.

My Dad, Art Schaefer, is the perfect father and role model and is a true American Hero. He flew 27 combat missions on a B17 during WWII and lived to NOT tell about it.

He was born and raised on a ranch in Wickenburg, Arizona ninety years ago and just surviving this was no small feat. He lived through the Great Depression and just surviving this was no small feat. After his father died at a young age, he became the family breadwinner and man of the family, and surviving this was no small feat. He has traveled the world, been in unforgiving jungles, deep in underground mines, at high altitudes in Peru and seen hostile guerilla forces in Nicaragua, Peru and other primitive locations and just surviving this was no small feat. His incredible life experiences have served to help define who he is and who we are too.

He taught me many life lessons through his gentle, quiet and humble actions as a great husband, father, provider and friend. He lives the values of a true gentleman. He is our family's greatest cheerleader and lives for those around him to bask in the spotlight while he stands in the shadows always ready to catch us if we fall. He has profoundly influenced my life by how brilliantly he lives his. He inspires and challenges me by his passion for life, his love and devotion for his family, his tireless dedication to excellence and his boundless intellectual curiosity.

I love, admire and respect my Dad!

Your son, Richard

TALLY LU

She is a very important member of the family and our PARTNER in life that adds joy, peace and love with every new day.

"AND GOD CREATED THE

HEAVENS AND THE EARTH,

AND THE LABRADOR THEREOF".

By Gene Hill

EPILOGUE
A LIFE SO RICHLY LIVED

Thank you everyone who has shared a part of themselves to make our whole life an adventure and a journey of challenging hills to climb and meadows to linger at, and ponder our many successes and blessings of a GREAT LIFE!!!

Art and Mary Esther

"WE HAVE WALKED TOGETHER IN THE SHADOW OF A RAINBOW."

American Indian Lore

ACKNOWLEDGEMENTS

My wife, Mary Esther, for working hard to make my long-awaited book, "In Like Flynn", come to fruition. Her devotion and dedicated belief that this book had to be written to tell and complete that cycle of my life, has been her goal and aim in life.

John Davis—A dear and caring friend who also felt the story of my missions must be told and shared. His deep interest in my Mission Diary and our friendship has motivated us to ask him to write the FOREWORD of this book. Mary and I thank John for his time, love and caring.

Laura Davis—A friend who has dedicated herself to spearheading this book going into print with the aim of making it a wonderful success.

Laura O'Bagy—Our dear friend and editor who has gone beyond sheer professionalism and has used her heart and knowledge to guide us.

Carolyn Davis—For her support and interest as both an accomplished author and good friend.

John Casey—Our loving son-in-law who has helped Mary through another book and helped her cure every computer snag possible to see this book through.

Richard Schaefer—For our grandson and accomplished teenage artist who has contributed his talents and creative paintings of airplane angels for his grandfather's book.

Arizona Lithographers—For always doing a superb job.

Hannah Haley Morris—A graphic design artist who used her skills to create the book layout and design with a dedication to excellence.

Photographic Works—Our friends, Mary Findyz, John Walden, Mick Landau, J.P. Westenskow, Carol Albee and all the staff who always approach their jobs with great personal interest in providing us with all the photos needed for my book and any other project we may be into at the time. They are always professional with expert knowledge, guidance and friendly interest.

Henry Sarnoff—Sarnoff Art and Writing Shop for always offering his professional advice and provided me with solutions. He's our dear friend.

Our Children—Nancy, Cheri and Richard for contributing their feelings of love for their Dad. They are our cherished accomplishments.

Frank and Willy Van Veenendaal—Contributing their story and feelings of being teenage recipients of the Food Drop over Holland during the German Occupation in World War II and becoming our dear friends 60 years later in the United States in a most bizarre and fortunate happenstance.

Mary Driscoll—Widow of Art Driscoll, the pilot I flew home with. She enthusiastically and unselfishly shared memories of her husband during his tour of Europe.

Juanita Hake—Widow of Bob Hake, our tail gunner. She kindly and unselfishly shared her husband memories and photos of his tour of Europe.

The Stars and Stripes—newspaper of the armed forces during World War II.

To our dear friends and family for all their encouragement and devotion.

ARMY AIR CORPS SONG

Off we go into the wild blue yonder

Climbing high, into the sun

Here they come, zooming to meet our thunder

At 'em boys, giv'er the gun, giv'er the gun now!

Down we dive, spouting our flame from under

Off with one helluva roar!

We live in fame or go down in flame,

Hey! Nothing'll stop the army air corps!